Hosted by God
To Really Live

Hosted by God
To Really Live

$\downarrow$

JENNI HO-HUAN

RESOURCE *Publications* · Eugene, Oregon

HOSTED BY GOD
To Really Live

Resource Publications
An Imprint of Wipf and Stock Publishers
199 W. 8th Ave., Suite 3
Eugene, OR 97401

www.wipfandstock.com

PAPERBACK ISBN: 979-8-3852-6003-4
HARDCOVER ISBN: 979-8-3852-6004-1
EBOOK ISBN: 979-8-3852-6005-8

Default Scripture References: NASB 1995
Other versions: NIV, The Message, New Living Trans.

"Pastor Jenni's vulnerable witness to God's gracious hospitality in her life can make each of us more courageous not only to open our hearts before the Lord in prayer, but to allow God to open his heart to us and wash us with his love."

—ANN GARRIDO, Associate Pastor of Preaching and Pastoral Theology, Aquinas Institute of Theology, St. Louis, Missouri

"City pastor Jenni Ho-Huan has written a beautifully contemplative book that explores the tension between our achievement-oriented culture and God's invitation to rest in his provision. In it, she offers a refreshing perspective on Christian spirituality that moves beyond performance-based faith toward a relationship of deep trust and authenticity with a God who welcomes us as we are."

—AARON LEE, Co-founder, Laniakea Culture Collective

"*Hosted by God* is a gentle and honest book. Through stories, prayers, and poems, Jenni invites us to see God not as distant, but as a gracious host. This book does not try to impress with loud or ostentatious ideas but offers quiet space for reflection and healing. Some may demand clearer answers, but others will welcome the chance to pause, listen, and be met by God in the midst of everyday life."

—LEOW WEN PIN, Associate Pastor, Bethany Evangelical Free Church

"In a style befitting St. Augustine's Confessions, Jenni shares so many insights from the trenches that resonated with me as I too struggle in the unconventional path. In the wisdom of her years, Jenni gives words, language, and stories to embody and enflesh what we have tried to express. Jenni's many thoughts on Christian hospitality are a refreshing beam of sunlight, like a morning window opened onto a cloistered living room. For anyone considering opening up their homes to host and welcome those in need of a safe refuge, this is a battlefield manual you must read. And for those feeling spiritually homeless in the midst of their missional calling, this is a precious friend to cheer you on. May the Lord use this book to help fan and fertilize a new wave of hospitality ministers and ministries to the nations in the days ahead."

—ABRAHAM YEO, Homeless Hearts and Youth With A Mission, Singapore

"Jenni lives the rhythm of what she writes—inspirational, intentional, invitational. The divine host and healer invites us to be hosts and healers in his likeness. Jenni exemplifies this in her hospitality as she invites you to find healing in these pages."

—TIMOTHY KHOO, Sojourner Guide, Desert Odyssey

"This book is a gentle companion for weary hearts. Jenni writes with honesty, warmth, and deep faith—reminding us that God's hospitality meets us right where we are. I found myself slowing down as I read, drawn into a quiet space of grace, love, and reflection."

—GOH WEI LEONG, Co-founder, Healthserve

"Filled with raw and funny stories, this part theological reflection and part practical guide uncovers the transformative power of God's hospitality and shares life's greatest invitation: to be hosted at God's Great Banquet, where we are warmly welcomed by the host despite our brokenness, complaints, achievements, and other false qualifiers. Hospitality thus becomes the ultimate safe space, an inclusive experience of genuine acceptance where we fall into grace and are loved. A thoughtful and provocative read for anyone wishing to experience this transformative joy and offer their life as a life-giving space for others."

—MELISSA ARATANI KWEE, Neighbor, Host, Steward

Contents

CONTENTS

Acknowledgements

No endeavour is ever a solo effort.

I am ever so grateful for the ecosystem God cobbled together that gave me the courage and resources to host this message and see it through.

Thank you *In.habit* team for saying yes to a new adventure and bringing your best: Joanna Tan, Aletheia Chan, Aaron Lee, Louise Yong and Joanna Lee, plus the artists and friends who contributed: Amelia Pan, Wong Kae Chee, Calvin Chong, Madeline Chu-Ang and Joseph Lee.

Collegeville Institute has been a special space that helped me rest, research and respond to God's call to investigate and communicate what I find. Back in Singapore, two other spaces allowed me to focus on the ideas and words, thanks to Goh Wei Leong's Halton Hideaway and the quiet home of Sam and Mee Ing Lim.

As the words tumbled out, some young adults indulged this aunty and read the unwieldy first draft: Isabel Chan, Abigayle Huan, Elly Chiu and Celina Eu. Later, Anne Chua my cousin via marriage took time to read and return with pages of feedback. I am grateful for your keen eye and honest feedback.

Incorporating poetry would be impossible except for my poet friends who understood the value and gamely contributed their precious pieces to help shed light on the message.

Fuel came from the divinely timed encouragement from readers who continue to interact with my older books and new ones who pick them up. Social media can be so helpful this way.

ACKNOWLEDGEMENTS

My cat Chats did her muse duties when she felt like it, but my family whatever they were feeling, gamely left me alone when I needed to hack through the jungle of ideas, feelings and words. Thanks dears.

Also, thanks to Media Associates International for its support for this book and for partnering gospel communicators globally.

Above all, thanks Abba for reassuring me that we are doing this together.

Prologue

An Invitation

This is a book of real stories, scriptural reflections and good poetry. This combination is intentional.

Most of us are used to a frantic pace, where we read fast to scan for vital information, take down bullet points and conclude that we have become wiser. In this way, the truths of life can slip us by because we presume to know them already. So, it is probable that we often miss what is important and vital.

This is where age helps. Growing older and facing many of life's surprises humbles us. Hopefully, we become more teachable as we discover that even basic things like friendship and kindness are far more layered than we realize. The way we discover this is through listening to other's stories and examining our own. Each of our lives is, in fact, an unfolding story.

Linking the virtue of hospitality with God is a discovery that took years—and age—for me to grasp. It involved slowing down and being vulnerable to move away from my own narrative about life, vocation and satisfaction. As I did so, I began to engage familiar Scripture texts afresh, and found some startling insights that freed me from my worn ways of seeing and doing life. This required me to adopt a posture of openness, and I encourage you to do the same as you read this book.

Something that helped me lower my guard was poetry. I was initially shy of poetry. After the clumsy experiences I had in school and the poor grades I received in class, I worried that I could not understand it. However, I soon learnt that poetry is not meant to be treated as a comprehension exercise but as a gift to awaken our imagination and longings. One cannot read a poem in a hurry. Poetry requires us to slow down and pushes us to relate and think more deeply. It helps us to notice, attend to, and appreciate the atomic nature of things where the power to recognize truth and make change lies.

I hope that as you journey along through the stories and insights in this book, you will find your heart and mind ignited in fresh ways that will enable you to live differently, with more peace and freedom. At the end of each section, there is space for you to pause and ponder and record your own feelings and discoveries. May you see that it is possible to live and thrive, no matter where you find yourself, as you embrace the truth of God's hospitable goodness.

EN(ter) into JOY!

At God's Table

The Lord is my shepherd, I lack nothing.
  He makes me lie down in green pastures,
he leads me beside quiet waters,
  he refreshes my soul.
He guides me along the right paths
  for his name's sake.
Even though I walk
  through the darkest valley,
I will fear no evil,
  for you are with me;
your rod and your staff,
  they comfort me.
You prepare a table before me
  in the presence of my enemies.
You anoint my head with oil;
  my cup overflows.
Surely your goodness and love will follow me
  all the days of my life,
and I will dwell in the house of the Lord
  forever. (Psalm 23, NIV)

I committed the beautiful words of this psalm to memory as a teenager, thinking I had mastered a portion of holy writ. But letting the words about God's goodness roll off my tongue isn't adequate. To know and live the truth take much more.

Truth never grows old. Instead, it calls us to grow up—and it grows along with us.

The words of Psalm 23 capture the full range of life's experiences, from the good times to the dark and awful ones. As the writer reflects on it all, he concludes with two statements: a sense of goodness and love pervades his life, and he has a home with God.

If this psalm describes how life is felt and lived, most of us are foreign to it. Can this truly be our experience too?

***

The soothing, lilting sound of a harp greeted each participant as they entered the Zoom Room, helping them to settle down. When it was time to begin, the manager shifted the spotlight to me and I welcomed everyone to *In.habit*—an online space for wounded and weary souls. I had felt God say during the COVID-19 pandemic: "Build a house for the lost and hurting," and this was our response. We had come together as a team to offer a safe space for others to feel their sorrows and to allow God to come close in His mercy and love, but it was a risky venture.

Singapore is a place where real estate is prized, and there was no way I could afford to rent a physical space. However, I also had no doubt, especially amidst the global crisis, that many were hurting. As people became more familiar with being online, I wondered about curating an online space of some kind. But what would we do? God hadn't said to offer a program but a 'house', a habitation. This meant a certain kind of environment, one of welcome and safety.

Over the years, I have felt the limitations of our often cookie-cutter ways of talking about God and life, and leading people into genuine spiritual encounters. We have relied almost exclusively on left-brained impartation of truth, where people sit passively and take in what is shared. There has been little attempt to engage the other half of our brains or to create a more dialogical, reflective exchange that could result in a more wholesome interaction and experience.

Right-brained approaches seem to me to be an entirely unharnessed gift, particularly as we speak of a God who is magnificent, glorious and beautiful. Our reluctance to incorporate the creative arts may be in part due to the shame we felt in our first messy attempts at any kind of artmaking in school. I find that so many of us, even artists, are convinced that we are not the 'creative sort'. Yet we all know what it feels like to be deeply touched by beauty, whether it is a sublime sunset or a mesmerising painting. As humans, we have a creative dimension within us that responds to that which is not primarily rational; there is great power in art. Indeed, art is a transcendent experience.

Also, as the typical experience in church is mostly one-directional, delivered from the stage, it tends to entrench the idea that those who lead are 'experts' while the rest of us are consigned to a struggling grasp of the spiritual. There is little space or empowerment for each of us to articulate our stories and little scope to fit them into the larger fabric of the faith community—unless they are shiny stories of success.

When I started building *In.habit,* I had an inkling that this house for the lost and hurting needed to incorporate fresh elements and take a new approach. I set up a chat group with some friends from different churches who I felt may have an interest in something like this. A good number of them were full-time artists, while others had day jobs or were students. To my surprise, they responded enthusiastically. I had to reiterate that this would be a quiet job with no remuneration and that it would require them to pray and prepare.

The team consisted of 'shepherds' and artists and a main facilitator. The 'shepherds' would hold space, listen and offer prayers in small groups, while the artists brought music, poetry and stories that helped create a sense of exploration and wonder. As the main facilitator, I wrote a script to weave the various elements together and create a cadence so that the participants could be gently led through openness, vulnerability and encounter in the ninety-minute session.

In my preparation, I saw a vision of a long table where many gathered for meals, which I recognized as a *Peranakan.*[1] At the head of the table was not the pastor, but God himself. My friends

---

1. Straits Chinese, who combine Malay-Chinese and Western cultures and developed a unique cuisine, patois, and cultural habits.

and I would bring our small dishes of loaves and fish, but the meal itself would be served by God. The team resonated heartily with this picture and approach. We committed to the value that since each of us is made in the image of God and holds great worth, we would focus on the people and not fixate on numbers or outcomes.

At the debrief after our first session, someone reported that when we offered a time of silence, a guest had seen a picture of the very same scene—a long table with God at the head. This was a tremendous encouragement to her, as she had never previously seen a vision in her faith journey. As a team, we were also overjoyed to hear this, as this was our first attempt acting as co-hosts at God's table. This shifted all of us toward a new way of doing things.

The 'easy yoke and light burden' of Jesus (Matthew 11:30) became real as we dreamt and worked, and I found myself learning to undertake ministry in a way I had never experienced before. I no longer resorted to cajoling, repeated pep talks, or emotionally psyching myself or the team.

I still marvel at the way the team was gathered and worked so well together even though most of us were new to each other. The heart connection we felt as we prepared was so sweet and hope-filled. God, the host, made sure the table was lavishly set. For example, as we prepared for the first session, the harpist and I soon realized that it was not easy to pick up the timorous sounds of the instrument over a laptop microphone. Neither of us was technically savvy, yet seemingly out of the blue, she connected with a relative who was able to help her set up with a proper microphone. At the end of that first session, we were surprised to find participants not just from Singapore, but from as far away as Croatia and Pakistan—all hearing the sound of the harp with perfect clarity.

So much of what I have learnt and become convinced about regarding life and faith crystallized for me through this 'risky experiment' of hosting people in the presence of God.

A core belief for Christians is that life is a gift and each of us is being matured into the kind of humanity Christ showed us. We speak of being "like Christ" which includes living in dependence and obedience to God our Father. In Jesus' own words, he did only the things that he saw his Father doing (John 5:19). This means that before any of us is involved or working for good, God already is, and it is in observing the ways of God in our world that we will figure out our part in it. I had preached on this, using the business analogy of God as the CEO or the boss, while we are the junior partners. But the mechanics of this escaped me until we built *In.habit.*

There was an "unforced rhythm" (Matthew 11:29 (MSG)) and I enjoyed such deep satisfaction. In my moments of quiet, it felt as if I had become a different person as a result of leaning into this approach. Slowly, I realized that this was not just another idea or task God wanted me to undertake, but a whole new way of being in the world.

While this felt momentous, I knew it could end up as mere formula unless I unearthed the true nature and extent of God's gracious hospitality towards us.

The Trail of Discovery

Life is not easy. This is why speaking about God, and blessings can easily sound hyper-religious, disconnected or even trite. Perhaps you find yourself scoffing at the very notion of God. You may have been deeply traumatized by someone who claimed to represent Him. Or perhaps you feel you have been dealt such a bad hand that you are left in utter despair, wondering if goodness could grace your life ever again.

My realization about the nature of God as a gracious host grew precisely through times of depression and looming despair. There were extended episodes of grief when I lost two of my dearest people within three years. There were disturbing existential questions when I could not understand why God did not intervene in situations where justice seemed perverted. There were ongoing challenges in daily life, with my marriage that did not feel like a 'happily ever after' and the struggles of parenting a neurodivergent child.

But my trudge through life turned a corner when during a time of prayer, I 'saw' a ray of light that bathed me and drew me in. It made me cast a fresh glance at the way I had come. I looked back at my journey and found that there was more to my story than I had noticed before. Like all stories, the plot developed, and the characters deepened when I began to include easily missed details.

I noticed new experiences emerging that I could not have arranged. I realized some stubborn relational patterns showed signs of change. I began recording instances of sheer providence. As I kept looking, the light's rays extended back across the years, and a new hue settled upon my terrain and gave my journey a more nuanced feel.

These revelations don't just apply to my story. I have found similar dynamics in the stories of others I have been privileged to know or be a part of, and in the stories recorded for us in Holy Writ.

***

My ruminations led me to wonder about the uniqueness of our common home, the earth. It remains the only habitable site we know of in the expanding universe. As it turns out, incredible precision is needed to sustain life here on planet Earth.

The earth rotates in a stable, predictable fashion. It has the exact chemical compositions and processes to support life. Even the ebb and flow of the tides are maintained by the faithful orbit of the moon.

The facts point to intelligent design. But life is more than design. It is *desire*. It is our desire to survive and thrive that drives all that we do.

But could our desire be rooted in another's desire—*for us?* After all, a designer does not have to create intricate conditions that support life. Earth's realities suggest that its designer is more a lover than an engineer or architect.

The Bible describes the beginning of time and life as we know it as an intentional act of God. His utterances brought the world and everything in it, into being. The book of Genesis takes us on a rhythmic account of the dawning of time and the emergence of flora and fauna, each life form more complex than the one before. Then it describes the creation of humankind.

At this point, the tempo slows and the wide-angle lens shifts to a close-up as God gets hands-on in the creation process:

> *The LORD God formed a man from the dust of the ground and breathed into his nostrils the breath of life, and the man became a living being.*
>
> Genesis 2:7

This first human being, bearing God's image, is placed in a lush garden, an environment God had already filled with vegetation that was both nutritious and a visual feast. This verdant, generous and unmerited provision was paired with a call to embark on the care of the garden and to submit to a specific boundary—the man was to avoid one particular tree, the "tree of the knowledge of good and evil" (Genesis 2:17).

The early chapters of Genesis show us that created in the image of God, we were meant to thrive and not just survive. Not only was there abundant provision; there was also the capacity to act upon our environment to make it flourish.

As the account continues, we get even more insight into God's desire for human thriving.

First, the animals were brought before Adam to be named, an act that signified knowledge and relationship. But none of the animals were suitable as companions. God then performed a tender surgical procedure, creating a woman. When God personally presented this wondrous gift to the man, he marveled at their likeness, and the two formed a procreative unit.

Unlike other creation myths and stories, Genesis reads more like a tender memory of a loving process of provision and relationship.

Alas, this idyllic scene was soon shattered by the decisions the first couple took. Using their power of choice, they defied God's boundary and, upon the urging of the enemy, partook from the tree they were explicitly told to stay away from. This act set in motion a whole different trajectory for humankind. From then on, their very existence would involve scrabble and strife.

The initial freedom they enjoyed was lost.

Instead of being able to revel in each other freely, Adam and Eve reached for leaves to cover themselves up, for now they felt the sting of shame regarding their vulnerability. Their thoughts and speech quickly turned towards judgment and blame. God gently helped them take ownership with His question: *Did you cross the line?* But their response was totally defensive. Instead of owning their part, they blamed each other . . . and even God. We see this in Adam's retort:

> "*The woman* you put here *with me—she gave me some fruit from the tree, and I ate it*" Genesis 3:12, emphasis mine.

Adam and Eve looked upon each other, and even on God, as an enemy to their welfare.

Other consequences soon reverberated. The original responsiveness of the ground would be thwarted by the competing growth of unfriendly flora. The woman's anatomy, while intact, would function thereafter with great pain.

The sense of harmony in the first ecosystem was shattered, and the intrinsic trust between God and humans was seared by a sense of alienation. No wonder we become strangers to ourselves, struggle to trust others, and feel like God is distant and foreign. Our endless desire for knowledge propels us, but it does not necessarily bring us the freedom and love we were made to enjoy.

As a pastoral leader, a wife, mother, woman and human, the reality of this sin-wracked world soon moved from a cognitive recognition to an embodied experience, and I discovered how elusive my preferred outcomes were.

Across the years and in many contexts, I have found others, both men and women, who confront these same existential and spiritual realities. Our efforts don't seem to pay off, the church can be a source of deep pain, and our cherished dreams can shatter.

In my attempts to sense-make, I journalled copiously. Over the years, I found that my story has two kinds of dog-eared pages. I am a little embarrassed to say it, but my brain, designed to protect me, at times loves to revisit the pain and continues to dig around for clues so I won't make the same mistakes again. I have found that this cerebral and emotional backtrack rarely serves me well. I guess this bears witness to the truth that what our first parents digested from the Tree of Knowledge is a part of all our DNA. We continually hope there is a vital piece of information that can save us.

But there are also pages that mark critical moments in my journey. I return to these pages to remind myself how I moved forward or persisted, often in surprising ways. These pages also reveal times when I was able to know what was truly going on and thereby find the clarity I needed to take the next step. Sometimes they record how a change in circumstances urged me forward to take a leap of faith.

Raised in a fast-paced, performance-oriented city and church, it took me many years to appreciate that the dark nights and hard treks that slowed me down were a gift. Times of grief, wounding and uncertainty often turn our gaze inward, allowing us to pay attention to the movements of the soul, the resources we have or lack within us. They make us question our assumptions and unsettle our pride. When our world feels like it's being deconstructed, our previously confident edifice called *Self* is often shaken to its core.

Unable to charge ahead, I began to experience how our *being* is a form of *becoming*. If I persisted in demanding the smoother paths I prefer, I may not have developed and grown in the way I needed to.

What is more wondrous is that I saw how in every season and episode of life, there was a supply that made a life of faith and fruitfulness possible. Some may call this 'luck' or 'fortune', but the precise timing, the exact amounts of financial provision, and the perfect way it fitted me and led me to growth, made it seem intentional and not random. It brought me back to how God created humanity and the way we were designed to live.

The first song in the Bible's psalm collection describes a tree that flourishes in all seasons:

> He will be like a tree firmly planted by streams of water,
> which yields its fruit in its season. Psalm 1:3

In the creation account, the earth was watered with streams or mists, and the first human was handmade from this watered ground. Funnily, we are eighty percent water—we learn as little schoolkids how important hydration is to life.

The moments of grace, providence, rescue and empowerment are like water to my soul, keeping me alive. *Where is the source of all this water? What if God not only sends out mercy and goodness but indeed designed us to feed and flourish only as we depend on this supply?*

God the Creator and Giver has generously set up a flow to nourish and care for us, like a good host. He wants the gift of life to be lived and shared and reproduced despite all the odds within and around us.

We are not meant to be the masters of our lives. We thrive when we learn to receive humbly and trust in The Host of life to provide.

This means we need to learn to pay attention to *where* God regularly waters us so that we are no longer thirsty and desperate. And perhaps we are meant to gather and undergo a transformation together so that our changed lives can encourage others and bring hope and healing to our broken world.

Soak & Savor

- *How did the story of In.habit make you feel?*

- *Have you ever felt a nudge to do things differently?*

  Which area of your life was that?

  What was your response and why?

- *What trails of discovery have you been on that have helped you to feel grateful for life?*

The best and most beautiful things in the world cannot be seen or even touched — they must be felt with the heart.

—HELEN KELLER

PART 1

Reconsidering The Way We Do Life

Many of us are raised to grab, rush and strive. As I was finishing school, many adults tilted their heads in my direction to remind me that 'it's a jungle out there'. This piled on top of other cliches, such as 'get a foot in the door', and there isn't enough pie for everyone so it's 'first come, first served', and that we don't know who we can trust in our 'dog-eat-dog world'.

The net effect of these popular dictums is a pervasive faulty belief that life is marked by scarcity and danger.

I once shared a story about how some beautiful postcards I bought on my travels which I had meant to send out invariably remained in my drawer. After a time, the envelopes stuck together and created a small mess while the moment of thoughtfulness passed. Funnily, a few I shared this with said it was their experience too. Don't we all find this tussle real—we want to be generous, but we hold back, and at times we even wonder if it's safe or worth it to give and share.

Besides the pervasive influence of such cliches, we are impacted by the choices we make as well as those made by people who influence or have authority over us. A good example of this is in partnerships where we went along with decisions which we may not have felt completely aligned with. When the outcomes were not what we hoped for, it made us upset at ourselves and at those who had the final say. Mistakes and regrets like these often lead to internal struggles where we feel paralyzed when we encounter divergent paths. In some instances, we may feel stuck with no way out, because we have given our word and signed on the dotted line.

Against these, we see in the Bible a God who opens doors, provides, grants favor, and said that 'the last shall be first'! When Jesus sends his disciples out on their first mission in pairs, he even tells them not to bring an extra 'backups' of clothes[1]!

There seems to be two diametrically different approaches to life, relying on ourselves versus relying on God. One view of life pits us against each other and constantly demands more from us so that we must hustle. The other calls us to a different risk venture.

Gently and over time, I understood that my view of God and life is often a clumsy mix of what I have been taught and how I have made sense of my experiences, and they were not often very coherent or integrated. These ideological clashes hit home when they become existential crises.

God had been using both the light and dark moments to urge my soul to explore something I never thought of before. The truths I glimpsed turned out to be utterly life-giving, freeing me from the beliefs built on scarcity and danger.

As you read on, think about your view of life. Consider too if you have been given an opportunity to rethink it.

---

1. Matthew 20:16, Matthew 10:10.

Mostly, not winning at life

Life can feel like a series of ongoing battles to be fought. Many times, we cannot even tell if we are winning or losing.

My parents, like most couples, had serious differences, and harbored disappointments. The latter must have run deep for my mom, because shortly after we moved to a larger flat, she refused to share the bedroom with my dad. In private moments, she has blurted out her suspicion that my father would have been a philanderer if he had the guts and the cash. Seeing as he sired eleven of us, she may not have been wrong.

Did she win by putting her foot down or did they both lose?

As a child, I hung on to the hope that my parents would be happy together. When I got to university, things got better and there was a thaw in their relationship when they separately started going to church. A few of us even persuaded them to take a vacation on their retirement. The first and only trip they had taken was a two-night tour up Genting and Cameron highlands in Malaysia. I was ten then, and it was my first time out of the country too. Only four of us went, for the trip was paid for by my older sister who had started working as a nurse. That trip, I watched them up close and became cognizant of their unhappiness. At a stop, I saw the first cow in my life and excitedly hopped off the bus with younger sister, our simple Kodak camera in hand. When we clambered up the bus to our seats, I found that they could not agree if we were safe or not, and so remained grumpily in their seats.

Nearly twenty years later, they were finally able to enjoy the luxury of a visit to my sister who lives in Perth, and they seemed open and even desirous of it. But that trip never materialized. One evening, after coming back to my seminary campus, I received a call that the police had come to inform us of our father's death.

I boarded the train home, enveloped in a surreal haze, unable to feel or think my way through the information I just received. After running up two flights of steps, I found the door shut as if no devastating news had just come through it. My younger sister who was alone at home came to the door and showed me the note the police left and said that we were to go to the hospital as soon as possible. My head spun. We made our way downstairs wishing our mom was around yet wanting to shield her from this. Just as we came out of the lift, we met our mom coming out of a taxi after her vacation. Soon, my mother, younger sister and I found ourselves on our way to the hospital to identify his body. That night, I heard for the first time, my mom howling in deep grief.

After that, three more sudden deaths followed, each different, across three generations, in my family. Each death dealt a blow to dreams and permanently changed the texture of our lives and our futures.

***

Death comes in other forms too. Dreams, hopes and plans die too.

Who does not hope for a full life? I became a pastor at age twenty-seven, ready to shepherd and grow my congregation to become a beacon of light and love. There was a lot to navigate as a single woman, trying to start a youth ministry, plan the pulpit and address very diverse needs within the congregation. I wondered what metric to use to evaluate my efforts and measure the outcomes.

Already prepared to remain single (who would want to marry a pastor?), I was surprised to meet Phil and have him besotted with me in my final year at seminary. Our match was a grand delight to many, and we had a huge wedding where two congregations, with distinct theological histories gathered to witness our union. Yet marriage would prove a hard, demanding ground that occasioned many deaths for the both of us.

Our august efforts to serve God often ran aground and we found ourselves taking roads less travelled, feeling isolated and lonely without our usual collegial connections.

Raising children brought about further challenges as our approaches and at times values did not dovetail.

I felt wearied by a daily sense of sadness and the uncertainty of the future. The usual narrative we have been taught in church is to progress from 'glory to glory' and 'strength to strength', to expect an upward trajectory of blessedness as we work hard and exercise faith, where dips and setbacks will make us stronger. My story felt more like long dark nights, tears that did not seem to stop coming, and harrowing thoughts that plunged me toward a spiral of discouragement. The pull to quit was real and at times felt promising.

Each of us weaves a specific garb that tells us what is right, wrong, acceptable or damnable. We construct systems of beliefs and behaviors to be approved and applauded. We intrinsically know how to put leaves together to protect ourselves and to make our way through life. Some of us people-please, some of us rebel, some of us hide, and some of us grind endlessly seeking perfection. These serve us well until things don't go quite according to plan. It always happens too that life will serve up curveballs. Death in its many permutations come at us. The leaves may feel like they are falling or are being ripped off.

We are frail and vulnerable to losses that can traumatize, wound, and scar us permanently. At such times, we can give in to cynicism and despair as it seems like nothing good lasts forever and we are so bad at loving, being kind, and generous.

I felt shocked, sad and ashamed that I seemed not to be adequate for this task called life. Beneath my bubbly personality lurked a melancholy that often darkened my days. My considerable education did not provide me with the answers to counter life's complexities. My strong faith commitment at times wavered for the God I trust is not a being I can see and explain.

Indeed, if life is seen as a ledger, I felt like a loser.

In the face of these realities, most of us soldier on as the only way we know, trying harder. Many of us break along the way.

But perhaps there is a wholly different approach?

Minnesota Interlude

In 2017, I flew halfway around the world to live in a cabin-like apartment by a lake called Stump. This was a gift that arose from the generosity of a monastic order, after a friend living in Canada recommended that I consider applying for a residency.

For a Protestant city girl, despite my deep admiration for monks and nuns and my personal growth through interactions with the writings of the desert fathers and mothers, living in an ecosystem framed and saturated by Benedictine values[2] was a different experience altogether which touched me at a visceral level.

I arrived to find a cabin that was equipped, clean and immediately livable. The staff, knowing I would be weary and hungry from my long journey, had set out some fruit and food for me, including bread that the monks routinely bake. The place was beautiful and peaceful, a writer's dream come true. When I wandered around the compound and read its history and work, my sense of wonderment kept growing.

I found my mind turning over what I have known all my life, and a hunger growing within me to know about the notion of hospitality, something frequently referred to as it was core to the Benedictines' ethos.

I recalled that through the entire process of application, they did not make me feel that I had to compete for a space or that I would not 'qualify'. Instead, my main anxiety was about getting my visa from the embassy.

Having been raised in impoverished circumstances, I had never related the practice of hospitality as something I could do, conflating it with the common notions of largesse and expense. In some ways, my theological upbringing which largely described

2. The Benedictines is an ancient community begun by St Benedict of Nursia in the 6th cent. For a community to live well together, he developed a rule to guide their commitments and behaviors known as the Rule of St Benedict. This rule has gone on to influence many other communities that formed across the centuries.

the work of God in judicial terms did not connect with the idea of hospitality either.

In this expansive space and in sweet solitude, surrounded by the natural beauty of the woods, I felt within my bones that these few weeks would be more than a good respite and a beautiful memory. But having come from a busy, fast-paced city, I found myself feeling anxious as I could not figure out how to translate such a different experience back home where the approach to life is vastly different.

There was a prodding within my soul to lean into a new possibility: perhaps this will birth something new within me. Across the weeks, the first embryonic vocabulary for the universal longing of all human hearts to be welcome, to find rest from strife, and have a space to just be, slowly took root in my heart. Aren't these the conditions of acceptance that will enable us to explore what truly matters and create what is meaningful out of our lives?

This interlude imprinted something upon my soul that would continue to enfold me and urge me in new directions. I was being dislodged from my old ways of survival and being led closer to the spring that would adequately supply what I truly needed.

Just maybe?

It was a usual sultry afternoon in tropical Singapore. With some time on my hands, I picked up Chats my calico cat and settled into my rocking chair. Chats, being the prescient animal she is, clambered off before the bothersome question resurfaced in my mind: How did I end up so far from what I had hoped and worked for?

I had thought that I would work well as a team with my spouse, and we would be vocationally fruitful as pastors, being able to lead and mature a congregation to have a significant impact on our society. Instead, we struggled with adjusting to each other's workstyles, and by this time we had been associated with several churches and their implosions.

As soft tears fell, another recent encounter where I had met someone new and introduced myself as a pastor came to mind:

"O, a pastor! Which church do you pastor?"

"I don't pastor a specific local congregation now", I say with some unease as I search the other person's face for a hint of genuine interest. Invariably, the conversation lumbers awkwardly from this point and fizzles out. It is always difficult to describe what isn't mainstream.

Not fitting into a regular pattern is somehow always suspect. But the pain runs even deeper than that. When catching up with an old friend who is a church elder and sharing briefly about my meandering journey, she paused for effect, tilted her head slightly before tossing the grenade of a question,

"If you cannot stay on, could the problem be *you*?"

"I thought it may be too." I had responded, with sincerity.

She did not pick up on the struggle this entailed, but ended the conversation swiftly, triumphant that she had detonated something, and I stood there feeling like I had to pick up all the pieces of my heart.

Even among old friends, it seemed there was no place for anyone who may be a problem. These experiences added to the deep disappointments I already bore.

I cannot quite see my way past all the messy, thorny realities, and I feel even worse on days like these. The tears began to fall more furiously now as I leaned back into my rocking chair.

The strong rays of the sun that fell across the floor earlier had begun to wane and an evening cool began to circulate with the whirr of my fan. It felt like I may be entering a shaded space of safety and my sadness seemed to be gently held back from bursting the dams of faith.

I closed my eyes and saw an image of flour being sifted, in tandem with the rhythmic motion of my chair. My mind thought back to the words of Jesus:

> "Satan has demanded permission to sift you like wheat; but I have prayed for you, that your faith may not fail; and you, when once you have turned again, strengthen your brothers." - Luke 22:31-2

As my tired soul gazed upon the gentle flour falling through the air, the surprising sight of a gemstone greeted me. What an unusual thing this is. Questions started flooding in: could God be holding the sift, did the flour represent my life, and what may this gemstone mean?

This homely image suggests that God is preparing a meal and that the ingredients that seem ordinary can hold some amazing surprises. It has been true that although my journey has been far from easy or straightforward, it has still been interesting and often fruitful.

I had mourned the losses of community, paycheck, pastoral colleagues, and vocational guidance. Yet I was never deprived of what each of these was meant to provide. Friendships, finances, partners, and opportunities never ceased but presented themselves to me as I kept putting one foot in front of the other.

I think back to times when I needed comfort, and a surprising text would come and blanket me in the assurance that I am not forgotten. Or times when I believed in a course of action but felt too small and inadequate, but then an opportunity would arise to concretize the idea.

Most of us want a God who shows up like the superhero Shazam, zaps away our woes, brings down our enemies and cocoons us in a good life. Instead, God chooses to pour out lifegiving water to soften the hard shell of our hearts and slowly help it open to receive light and life. God patiently offers us breathing space, time, and resources, no matter how limited, to respond to His goodness, and to slowly emerge free and full.

The word 'hospitality' sprang to my mind. Memories of my sojourn in Minnesota returned, together with the sense of quietude and calm.

I felt like I had entered a clearing in a forest and saw for the first time the truth of what was going on. In a world of strife, selfoptimization, and labels, God had graciously taken such care of me despite my unusual path. These words from the Psalms rang truer in that moment:

> *My help comes from the Lord, who made heaven and earth. He will not allow your foot to slip. (Psalm 121)*

> *If the Lord had not been my help,*
> *My soul would soon have dwelt in the abode of silence.*
> *If I should say, "My foot has slipped,"*
> *Your lovingkindness, O Lord, will hold me up.*
> *When my anxious thoughts multiply within me,*
> *Your consolations delight my soul. (Psalm 94)*

As I rocked back and forth, physically going nowhere, I sensed that I was making strides in my spirit. God was ushering me into a new way of being, where I need no longer be the protagonist.

I would go on to find out that God hosts us in a variety of ways and that wondrous things happen when we become aware of his hospitality and respond to it. Stay on the trail with me as I share this discovery with you!

Part 1 Highlights

- *God's version of life contradicts the dominant narrative of struggle, strife and scarcity.*

- *A shift in our perspective may require new experiences and changes in our circumstances.*

- *God desires to reveal more of Himself and His ways to us.*

Soak & Savor

- *Has life felt like a battle for you, and how do you tend to handle these challenges?*

- *God took Jenni away from the familiar to help her see things in a new light. How has God done that in your life?*

- *What possibility might God be inviting you to lean into?*

- *Enjoy the poem at the end of this section and journal your thoughts and feelings.*

Charism

~ Desmond Francis Xavier Kon Zhicheng-Mingdé

To have something, yet not know—
how blessings come and go unnoticed.

Unacknowledged, like the providential;
who has forgotten the ever-present

gifts, the givenness, the giftedness?
But you look at your memory, its oldness.

And ask: how can your own humanity
forget so easily, disappoint so effortlessly?

Repeated motion, and movement again;
again is the refrain of the life of penance.

Again is the natural rhythm of meaning—
meaning can come and go, dissolve

and disappear, only to surface a wave.
Small emotion of hope, of crosses carried.

And love—it's always love—but again,
how we are reminded of its old presence

eternal
and always here

preternatural quiet

holding
space—

God's hand.

For I am your guest— a traveller passing through,
as my ancestors were before me.

PSALM 39:12 (NLT)

PART 2

God's Hospitality
and our Four Deep Needs

Since that moment on the rocking chair, I have been looking over my experiences to make sense of how God could be a host and discovered that we have some debris to clear first.

First, the word hospitality for most of us seems to be related to the idea of hoteliers and food and beverage (F&B) establishments. Secondly, we all have experiences where hospitality has been challenging.

The friend who means well but brings out all her fine China can make us nervous about breaking something precious. Or one could show kindness only to have the recipient interpret wrongly and the relationship becomes tense with unclear expectations. Then there are relatives we feel obligated to host. Who does not have the one aunt or uncle who pry too much, the cousin who has grown up and become aloof, someone who loves to tell stories and jokes that others deem a tad over the top, or another who eats too much and offers too little? Often too, especially as children, we have been told to dress or act or speak in certain ways, so as not to upset some person in the clan who held sway over the adults in some way.

All these experiences make us steer clear of hosting and being hosted, because of the ladened expectations that come with it.

Hospitality is an uncomfortable word and experience for most of us.

The idea that God is hospitable isn't something I have been taught or teach others. Rather, we are exhorted to be hospitable, which most of us find exceedingly difficult.

For most of us too, God is a perfect being who is far removed from our gritty realities, and although we hold faith in Him, we commonly harbor severe doubts about him: if He were hospitable based on our ideas of hospitality, He would use his might to put an end to all the suffering we witness and life would be one huge party.

Furthermore, I observed that the way we related to God vacillated between the poles of wanting to barge in and demand answers (and we sometimes do) and nervously keeping our distance while we figure out how we must first shape up before we can broach an approach. There is no ease even while we have access, and our generally private piety often conjures a God who deals with us in punitive and censorious ways.

All these very real struggles that are part of a life of faith are often tucked away from the light of honest conversation.

Could it be that God's presence and activity in my life was not fully in plain view and I did not know Him deeply enough to live the way he designed me to?

What if God is indeed hospitable?

As I challenged my understanding, read, prayed and thought about it more, I discovered what true hospitality is, its impact, and why it must begin with God, the Source of life. Indeed, to really live, we all need to feel safe and secure and to know that our lives carry significance. Our needs, when unmet, will send us rushing headlong into frenetic control or cause us to crash from overdrive. It is easy to see evidence of this all around us. Many live at the edge of burnout where peace is elusive and any delight or joy in life is outweighed by the drudgery and jabs of pain we feel.

God's hospitality meets our deepest needs. Through the healing and restoration that comes as we awaken to God's gracious hospitality, we will become more rooted and grounded through life's vicissitudes. These effects will be explored later in part four of this book.

First, let's explore the four dimensions of God's hospitality that meet our deepest needs in life.

1. Genuine Welcome

I left the cabin for a walk the abbey on the campus of St. John's in Collegeville and came to a concrete plaque with these words on it:

> *And let due honor be shown, especially to those who share*
> *our faith (Galatians 6:10) and to pilgrims.*
> ~ Rule of Benedict 53

Honor? My experiences are marked more by the times I have been slighted, ignored, and even betrayed—largely in contexts of faith no less. Heavy hearted, I walked to a bench next to this sign where an older lady was sitting and asked to share the seat. She moved to give me more space, and we started talking. Towards the end of our conversation, Bernadette looked me in the eye, smiled broadly and said, "Thank you for coming and for sharing your wisdom with us". I was struck by her words. She was not sharing the seat with me out of mere politeness. She was offering me a genuine welcome, where I mattered and may even bring a gift.

I realized then that hospitality does not consider the guest as a mere taker and it does not begrudge the giving, for it expects to receive. I think to the times Jesus shared spaces with others.

After a long journey on foot in a foreign, even hostile territory, Jesus decides to sit by a well near the noon hour. A woman, of poor repute comes to draw water. They begin to talk, and Jesus gives her the chance to host him by asking for a drink of water[1]. Such a request is unthinkable in that day for men did not openly mingle with women who were not related to them. Furthermore, the woman is a Samaritan, a culturally distinct group that the Jews

---

1. John 4:1–26.

belittle. Understandably, the woman is bewildered at his request and in her discomfort blurts out some theological cliché to try to throw him off. Little did she know that Jesus had made a planned detour to meet with her. He of course bores into her soul with penetrating questions and reveals that He is the real host here, as he offers her a drink that would permanently satisfy her ultimate thirst –

> "If you knew the gift of God and who it is that asks you for a drink, *you would have asked him,* and he would have given you living water." (John 4:10, emphasis mine)

Jesus did not operate by society's labels and stereotypes. With her multiple failed marriages, this woman would not experience welcome, and her appearance at the well at noon suggests that she is avoiding other women. But Jesus sat and waited for her to arrive and spoke of her life with tender understanding. He offered her a genuine welcome.

A genuine welcome does not disempower us, make us needy or reduce us to our gnawing needs. It takes our needs seriously, patiently shows us the greater need that lies beneath and offers us real salve, solace and solution.

This is the way God hosts.

In the encounter, the Samaritan woman felt seen. Jesus revealed His knowledge of her life and her longing for love. Instead of condemnation, His revelation brought her to an open space of authenticity. This is how the story ends –

> *Now many Samaritans from that town believed in him because of what the woman said when she testified, "He told me everything I ever did." So, when the Samaritans came to him, they asked him to stay with them, and he stayed there two days. Many more believed because of what he said. And they told the woman, "We no longer believe because of what you said, since we have heard for ourselves and know that this really is the Savior of the world. (John 4:39–42)*

Perhaps in our daily routines, Jesus similarly makes a personal trip to meet with us and wants to host us towards a freedom and life this world cannot offer.

2. Rest from strife

Naturally and intuitively, I turn to God whenever I need help, relief or answers. But God's response to our cry for help may take us by surprise. Two examples from Scripture show us this truth.

Paul had a persistent issue that bothered him and would not give him any peace. He described it as a thorn in his flesh, one so embedded that only a divine surgery could hope to relieve him of it.[2]

Yet as Paul, the great missionary and apostle who wrote more than half the New Testament canon, found out, God's answers can look very different from our expectations.

This is how he summarized his struggle:

> Concerning this, I pleaded with the Lord three times that
> it would leave me.
> But he said to me, "My grace is sufficient for you, for my
> power is perfected in weakness." (2 Corinthians 12:8-9, CSB)

Paul discovered that the paradox was to stop trying so hard, to desist, to learn to let things be, to rest from strife. As he did, a greater power took over:

> Therefore, I will most gladly boast all the more about my
> weaknesses, so that Christ's power may reside in me. So,
> I take pleasure in weaknesses, insults, hardships, persecu-
> tions, and in difficulties, for the sake of Christ. For when
> I am weak, then I am strong. (2 Corinthians 12:10, CSB)

Nearly a millennium earlier, another faith warrior had experienced the same.

2. 2 Corinthians 12:7–10

Elijah the prophet had boldly confronted the political big-wigs of his day and defeated them flatly[3]. In an all-out contest, he had summoned all the false prophets to a live match. They were to call upon their god to set an animal sacrifice ablaze. Those four hundred prophets launched into a sustained frenzy from incantation to lacerating themselves, but they saw no success. Elijah then made his own task harder by dousing his sacrifice with water that filled the trough around it. But God sent a fire that manifestly demonstrated his reality and power.

Although God showed up, this victory brought about a bounty for Elijah's head. He fled for his life, reached the limit of his endurance, and could not imagine going on with his diatribe.

> "I have had enough! Lord, take my life, for I'm no better than my ancestors."
> Then he lay down and slept under the broom tree. Suddenly, an angel touched him. The angel told him, "Get up and eat." Then he looked, and there at his head was a loaf of bread baked over hot stones, and a jug of water. So, he ate and drank and lay down again. Then the angel of the Lord returned for a second time and touched him. He said, "Get up and eat, or the journey will be too much for you." So, he got up, ate, and drank. Then on the strength from that food, he walked forty days and forty nights to Horeb, the mountain of God. (1 Kings 19:4–8)

Paul and Elijah are strong characters we often admire. Yet I noticed that as God welcomed them, allowing them to freely express their desperation and confusion, a rest comes over them and their brute strength is tempered by a divine touch of gentleness. Sometimes, a meal awaits afterwards.

In both these accounts, we find that God neither upbraided them nor minimized their suffering. Instead, God draws them away from the human instinct to seek comfort in explanation and resolution. He allows their hearts to ache and break open to receive the deeper truth they need. The hard things of life can be

---

3. 1 Kings 18:20–40

borne when we cease from striving to explain or contain them but rather allow God to strengthen us.

As we strive, we will bump up against our humanity, which is that we are finite, contingent beings designed to depend on God. Thus, only in turning to God and letting go of our reflexes will we be able to fully engage with the journeys we are on. And it often means to approach things very differently from what we were used to.

3. Space to be

While it is needful to be able to do things, and learn them in time, the 'doing' eventually overtakes the 'being' because this is what the world sees and celebrates. We are continually locked into states of action and often feel we have to justify our need for rest, hence we have #guilt hashtags. This exhausts us and forecloses the importance of simply 'being'.

For those of us who can afford it, the usual solution is to take a vacation, a break from all the 'doing' and its attendant expectations and deadlines.

But if our internal circuitry is so wired towards action, even our periods of rest can become simply another round of activity, a tendency abetted by our consumer mindset and competitive culture. Taking a break means purchasing novel stuff and experiences, often eagerly shared on social media. I used to chortle at my well-heeled church members saying they need a vacation from their vacation. But now I know how true that can be, for rest and recreation, renewal and rejuvenation come to us when we can simply - be.

This means that whether we travel or stay put, what needs to happen is an experience where we stop trying to justify or defend ourselves. It is when we don't have to feel shame or guilt for existing and taking up space. It is when, even though we don't have all the answers, we have a measure of peace.

This freedom requires either solitude or the company of a person or persons who do not need to make any claim on you. Both allow you to just be, without having to explain or adjust yourself. In our world of activity, we are led to think such freedom is a luxury. But when we realize that quality activity derives from a secure and unstifled sense of self, it becomes clear that this is a necessity.

Christians believe that we are creative beings, imaged after the Creator God. Our longing for transcendence, capacity for imagination, and our grand desires are all indicators of our spiritual and generative nature. I always wonder what the world would be like if everyone of us could experience the freedom to show up fully and be given the space to flourish.

Both artists and scientists agree that we need the twin poles of solitude and community for our well-being.

Solitude, while attractive, is extremely hard for all of us. Anyone who has attempted it knows that being alone may not foster the sense of rest one longs for. In fact, it will at first be a most uncomfortable, even intimidating experience. As we slow down, things we have ignored or repressed often surface. In solitude, one encounters the unhappy presence of the parts of us we dislike: our shadows, the tourbillion of unanswered questions, unresolved hurts, even haunting memories. I am often told by those who come to my retreats that they are nervous about being alone for extended periods of time or that they worry they will be unable to stop and enjoy the solitude. But as they dip their toes into a guided experience and stay with it, they are always amazed at the sense of rest they feel and the clearing they arrive at.

When we are with others, expectations creep in. Our compulsions and socialization make it hard for us to simply acknowledge another's presence and leave well alone. We will feel the need to talk, and act. It's so hard for us to simply be together, allowing each other to take up space and breathe the same air without laying claims or making demands.

God is uniquely able to offer us both solitude and community.

Since God knows every detail of our lives, including the back alleys of our motives and memories, He is the person before whom we need not contrive a conversation. Of course, the thought that God knows us so thoroughly unnerves most of us. But it is precisely this truth that allows us to shed all our pretentions and posing, and shift from a persona to a presence. This shift is crucial for us to come alive, as we begin to just be.

Margie had come to our 'Broken-hearted' themed *In.habit* session. During the breakout, when we simply asked why each had come, and allowed them to share to their level of comfort, she sounded so shattered that all she could offer was the word 'numb', and that she had not felt much variance emotionally for a while and was unable to shed any tears even when she wanted to be supportive of others. At the end of the session, she turned her camera on and shared that a tear had come as the harp played.

In offering a space for people to just be themselves, while we shared music, art and curated words, we repeatedly saw God encounter and touch different ones. Many also realized that instead of being punitive and harsh, God is the most companionable living presence we can lean into and enjoy.

It may not have occurred to us, but God is the One person who allows us the space to just be, with His genuine welcome and gentle ways, "for he knows how we are formed, he remembers that we are dust." (Psalm 103:14)

4. Challenge to live

We aren't just dust either, we are also stars:

> "... you will shine among them like stars in the sky"
> (Philippians 2:15b, NIV)

But many of us lose our shine and hide our light. We all have times of shame, times when we let ourselves down, times of struggle with failure and deep disappointment. For those who practice faith, we may continue with our faith acts and commitments, but a shadow has darkened the way, affecting our clarity and confidence. Perhaps this is why we can be our own worst enemy as doubts buffet us.

I was not expecting that with age, I would wrestle with more frailties, emotionally and spiritually. Some part of us assumes that with more knowledge, we would fare better as we go. This is especially so in our culture that prizes education, such that we can go for endless Bible Study courses to learn and gain more knowledge. Or we believe that as we achieve our goals, we will be happier. The reality is that new fears greet us with the seasons. Everything comes with its own set of issues and challenges.

Life is beset with many ways to get anxious and fearful. The young woman struggling to keep up with tasks at work, the star student who descends into depression, the popular and attractive young gal who self-harms and suffers from body image issues. So many of these may seem irrational to us and we are often impatient with them. But each of these mirrors for us how hard life can be and what we stand to lose when we don't have the resources to navigate the storms.

Our fears, anxieties, regrets, and dreads circle us like ravenous wolves, and our reflex is to shrink back. We may use avoidance, we may bang on pots, and we may run. None of these tactics will totally rid us of the wolves. They return. Wolves cannot be domesticated into pets, so we must beware of them. But if we allow the fear of their presence to overtake us, they will come to rule the terrain of our soul. When this happens, we will tend towards fretting, anxiety and worry, and the joy of life will be drained away from us.

In my times of weariness and confusion, grief and failure, I have relished how God bade me welcome and gave me a sense of respite in my times of solitude. Throughout, my preferred solution was for God to slap those wolves and send them groveling away. Instead, He let the wolves hang around and helped me to grow less fearful of them. Over time, He opened my eyes to how large the wolf population is and how many of us are wounded and encircled by them. God was challenging me to remember that since the beginning of time, I was made to rule over creation, and that even wolves can be subdued. Again and again, God moved me beyond where I was, graciously hosting me to the point where I was ready to hear His challenge to me to live large and brave in the face of these real and present stressors and difficulties.

A significant lesson is that the real danger lies in the fear the wolves create, more than the wolves themselves.

When I turned fifty, medical checks became more important. At one such investigation, a biopsy was called for. As my family history has an indication for cancer, the results could be positive. I thought to turn to the internet and friends who have gone through similar experiences for information and guidance. Even as I played the scenarios out in my head, I noticed that there was something more sinister than the disease that wanted to overtake me. It was fear.

Fear writ large can play with my mind and drag in other emotions that easily clutter my heart and dampen my soul. It is no wonder that the Bible pits these two states against each other: fear or faith.

Fear makes us numb and jittery. It causes us to shrink back or employ reactions and reflexes that do not serve us in the long run. In contrast, faith is a confidence that walks the plains of life not with naiveté, but with warrior-like capacities to anticipate and respond to difficulty with grit and often a smile.

God wants to host us toward this inflexion point: will we lean into faith or let fear grip us? The latter will hold us hostage and keep us stuck. Faith, on the other hand launches us on an adventure of discovery, growth and exploits.

Knowing that God would not disdain my concerns, I came before Him in prayer and named all my fears. I grieved over how aging comes with such difficulties. As I emptied myself of all the cares clogging my soul, memories began to float to the fore. As if sitting with an old friend going over photographs of the times we have shared, my heart began to quieten. Then an old tune with these words played in my mind –

> *He didn't bring us this far to leave us*
> *He didn't teach us to swim to let us drown*
> *He didn't build His home in us to move away*
> *He didn't lift us up to let us down*[4]

A peace settled upon me, and I decided that should a terminal disease become a part of my story, my posture would be to lean on God and go down the path with equanimity and not take my eyes off the needs of others around me.

We cannot 'will' ourselves to trust God more deeply. Trust is a relational quality that grows out of the soil of a growing relationship of transparency and openness.

We have inherited from our first parents a tendency to keep a distance from God. So, He pursues us with His hospitable ways till we turn from the way we do life to embrace life as a gift to be shared. Living with a dependence on God's trustworthiness will expand our soul, hone our capacities, and develop our ability to better assess the hard situations we find ourselves in.

---

4. 'He didn't life us up to let us down' by The Imperials in Heed the Call.

Part 2 Highlights

- Our commonly held ideas can prevent us from receiving the truths about God and life.

- We all need to experience genuine welcome, rest from strife, a space to be and a challenge to really live.

- Seen from the light of these needs, the stories in the Bible reveal to us that God is a gracious host.

- The Bible often juxtaposes faith and fear. Fear will keep us stuck and small while faith will cause us to embark on a more adventuresome approach towards life.

Soak & Savor

- What are your ideas of hospitality?

- Which of the four needs do you feel you lack most in your life now, and why?

- Where may God be inviting you to choose faith over fear?

- Enjoy the poem that follows and journal your feelings and thoughts.

prayer (xxi)

~ Jonathan Chan

in the turning and turning of
an unwanted grief, I saw the extension
of an old, familiar hand, shrivelled and
pruned. It took my palm, clenched it,
and helped it remain tender. Tender
enough to hold every interminable doubt,
every interminable sorrow. The prayers
moved through the columbarium. An
outpouring of loves that didn't know
they had somewhere to go. Tragedy
beckons to joy. Come for a while,
stay.

Hospitality is a tangible encounter with the grace of God

~ BOB EKBLAD

PART 3

Being Loved and Tasting Grace

Love is the most celebrated thing in popular culture. It's been said that love makes the world go round.

Then there is Grace, something we all need and desire in our lives.

Yet in our typical way of living—which is to manage, control and manipulate, love and grace become foreign and distant to most of us. Love is conflated with romance and pheromones which fade swiftly in the face of hardship and conflict. For many of us, grace feels like a soft option that gives a free pass to those we should hold accountable.

Love and grace do not direct or mark our lives. We march relentlessly towards our ambitions or are driven by our fears, whilst leaving in our wake broken hearts and dreams.

What if we have gotten it wrong, and life is meant to be lived around the power of love and grace?

Just as water is made up of hydrogen and oxygen, God's hospitality is the twinning of his love and grace flowing toward us.

Read on and see how this flow is present in your life, whether you are religious or not. As you notice the presence of the flow of Grace and Love, would you be open to seeing and doing life differently?

Grace, the *modus operandi*

When I was younger and figuring out life, I wished someone could have handed me a set of *Instructions for Life* that are always clear and prompt. Then my parents can follow these instructions and be happier and give us better guidance. Then I would know exactly what I need at every turn so that I don't mess up and hurt myself and others.

Were we all to have these instructions, we weren't all be scarred by so many wounds, battling so many shadows, and exhausted from watching our steps. What would life feel like if we could trust each other, be given the space to attempt things weird and wonderful, be accepted when we are different -- because it was all spelled out clearly in the instructions?

Sadly, this set of instructions does not exist.

If you are religious and have a text you go to, those texts are ancient and you still must make sense of what they mean before you figure out what they mean for you today.

Clearly, this thing called life requires some fight from us. In fact, it is precisely the battles that create saints and warriors. But there is help along the way.

Instead of outright instructions, we have the capacity to intuit information, what could be called 'hints. While there may be grand battles to engage in, most of our lives are compounded by smaller decisions we make. Here, the fight isn't always loud and obvious. Often, it is choosing to follow a hint, as a venture of risk, and finding that it can lead us to fuller revelation and trust:

Did that upset mom?

Perhaps there is another way?

Is there a great Something or Someone out there?

These hints show up in different ways. It can be a new question bubbling into consciousness. It can be a surprising new view we glimpse. It can be a stirring and longing that keeps hanging around going, 'Well?'. At times it feels more like an impulse—make that call, now.

Or it can feel like a premonition, a storm warning, so we can brace for it. Often, it's like a trail of crumbs and if we follow it, we find our way home.

The hint's alphabetical and ontological ancestor is Grace. Grace can come gently like a feather carried by the wind. It comes as moments of realization, indications, information and as opportunity. Each one is an invitation to notice, feel, consider, weigh and choose afresh.

Grace can also feel as total as a wrecking ball that can cause our cherished structures of beliefs and lifestyles to collapse. When sudden infirmity greets us, loved ones walk away, and when our usual securities unravel.

Where does Grace come from and what happens when we follow it?

How can we learn to detect its presence and activity?

What do we do in response so that it opens to a clearing of freedom, courage, and power for us?

Let's turn to a few stories for help.

***

The first is the well-known tale of The Good Samaritan.[1] This is a story told by Jesus to a religious leader who was keen to justify himself by delineating who is deserving and who is not. This is a tendency we all have, the way we divide the world into people who are deserving and those who we cannot be bothered with, for various reasons. Since Jesus spoke of loving our neighbor, his most natural question to Jesus was: who is my neighbor? In other words, who do I have to love?

The story Jesus proceeds to tell is anything but a sentimental one. There is the harsh reality of danger from bandits, being mercilessly robbed and roughed to the point of death.

---

1. Luke 10:30–37.

We are deeply relieved to find that someone does come along after two earlier ones bypassed the poor man, finally stops to help, and does so extravagantly.

My first reading of this was to wish that were I ever in the dastardly predicament as the poor man, a good Samaritan would come my way. Slowly, I admitted that rising to be some modicum of the Good Samaritan is an ethical demand. I should try to be as good as possible.

But the story refused to go away as it began to surface many more thoughts:

> *Why was the Samaritan able to be so good towards someone belonging to a group that regularly looked down on him?*
>
> *How devastating it must have been for someone who considered himself religiously and culturally superior to be in a place of such desperation to need help from someone he regularly disdains?*
>
> *What impact did it have on the innkeeper who must be mystified by the Samaritan's deed—getting all messed up, offering his animal, slowing down, sacrificing his resources including paying for bed and lodging until the man recovers!*

What must happen for centuries of animosity to fall away so that the Samaritan would bother to stop and go to such great lengths? Perhaps at some point in his own life, this Samaritan experienced and understood what terror and terminal hopelessness must have felt like. At some point in his own life, this Samaritan was offered and received mercy and aid. At some point in his own life, this Samaritan knew that what he owned are gifts for sharing and not hoarding. This is not the outcome of an educated or calculated process. Whatever led to his conviction and action can only be described as Grace. He has received it and is living in a way consistent with it.

This story illustrates how Grace is that illuminating gift that softens us and strengthens us to do the hard stuff.

The second story is set in a family. It is one of a set of three stories Jesus told to the mixed crowd listening to him: skeptical religious leaders, zealous followers and curious and needy men, women and children.

In this story, a younger son flagrantly demands his share of the family inheritance from his father, who is still alive, then goes and squanders it in wanton living[2]. He is hit by severe financial woes whereupon he finds himself in sudden, abject poverty. Far from home, he drags himself to a farmer who sends him to feed the pigs. There in the pig pit, he realizes his folly enough to reckon that his best hope is to return home as a servant. He had after all, relinquished his position as a son with his drastic and dishonoring choice earlier.

Meanwhile back at home, the wise father who is aware of his son's proclivities anticipates and hopes for his sorry return. True enough, one day, he spied the form of his son, all bedraggled and forlorn making his way homeward. The father, who is beside himself with joy, hikes up his manly garments and runs like an excited kid to greet and welcome the son home. In Jewish culture, such a son would be disowned by the entire village, unless the one he disgraced extends pardon first. So, the father runs.

It is easy to judge this son, and we often apply this judgment to others, angry at their sense of entitlement, irresponsibility, and outright disrespect. Turning to the father, most of us in positions of authority would feel this is 'a bit much'.

There are many angles to this story but at its heart, it is a story about all of us. Like this son, we cave in to the desire for immediate gratification that gnaws at our souls, distracting us from what we may already have. Isn't it a common problem that we all tend to take things for granted? At times, we may even spurn the good right before us because we insist that the grass is greener elsewhere. While our hearts are churning with all this envy and

2. Luke 15:11–31.

covetousness, the father figure, fully aware, refuses to remove our free will, but stands ready to receive us home.

This story shows us Grace as the tenacious offering of hope that allows for restoration and renewal.

**

The final story is from my life. I was at a writing residence and the director asked us to share something we feel comfortable letting the others know. I mistook her question for a writing prompt and wrote this:

> I'd like you to know what holds me together. Yes, the thing that threads and weaves and binds and runs through days, nights, howling wind and eerie silence. It tugs and pulls me back from the abysses and leashes and leads me forward toward the bright and the beautiful, the true and the trustworthy.
>
> I was nearly sold as a child, to a rag-and-bone man, a bachelor, who lived several floors below our tenement apartment. My mom took me outside our flat to the end of the corridor where we could see the floors below and asked me, the seventh of her nine children, "Would you be willing..."
>
> Something came and wrapped itself around our hearts. Asian parents do not go down on a knee to speak with their children and rarely offer direct eye contact except in fury.
>
> Our eyes met.
>
> I, the seven-year-old—before words could form to respond to her– was completely awash with relief as my mom got up and said "No".
>
> We never spoke of it again.

Recalling this, I realized that God had been present before belief, doctrine, and church.

Grace shows up as the intervention that interrupts a trajectory.

I know the word Grace is used a lot, and it is misunderstood a lot too. There is a simple reason for this. It is not natural to us, and humans are an impatient lot. When something is not familiar to us, we either dismiss it, or we caricature it.

Caricatures of Grace abound today:

- *"Show some grace," we say, which is to loosen up and not dig too deep.*
- *You have a 'grace period', which is to be given a bit more time to set things right.*
- *It's all Grace, a most enticing notion parried by some preachers, which is to give you a free pass on your true state of being.*

These caricatures are helpful in one thing: they tell us that Grace is something that we need at some point in our life.

None of this is Grace though. They seek to proximate it but are all fundamentally inadequate and flawed because we are dependent, contingent beings. Indeed, our need for God's Grace is full and final, form the first to the last breath

This being so, it should not surprise us that both anecdotal evidence and research has shown that those who are more affluent are at risk of developing bad habits of entitlement and weak theology. Jesus said it was hard for the rich to enter God's Kingdom, and in an exchange with a rich young ruler, the latter when confronted with how attached he was to his wealth, turned away for the paradigm that his wealth is all a gift of Grace was too foreign for him. He wrongly presumed that his wealth was a result of his inheritance or hard work, something he deserved and owned.

It is easy to confuse our pedigree, productivity, and personal charisma as sources of our good fortune. In effect, every single bit of it is Grace.

As Grace comes from a different plane than what we are used to, it takes intentional effort to notice it, learn its ways and co-operate with it. This means learning to slow down and become more alert to our lives. As a body-soul-spirit complex, we can receive hints of both the presence or absence of Grace from our bodies, our emotional states, our relationships and even our circumstances.

The persistent ache, the brewing resentment, the silent treatment, and the office gossip are all indicators that we have lost sight of Grace, and are operating from fear, anxiety and control. In this state, we are far from the gracious hospitality of God but have reverted to believing the lie that we are fully responsible for all outcomes. This stress takes up all our capacities and energies, and we end up skimming the surface of what is going on, which tends to make things worse as we react to seize control. We are not at our best, and the price is paid in our own sense of self, our relationships, and our vocational impact.

Grace is the modus operandi of Life. It is sheer grace that air moves in and out of our lungs.

Grace is Life's invitation to live the way God designed the world to instead of succumbing to our tyrannical and frightened approach of control and manipulation. Apart from it, we end up grinding.

Grace-filled living opens us up to gratitude, holding lightly, and hopefully, being gracious to others. We can experience a better integration of our minds and our bodies. Our emotions can become our servants that highlight deep needs that need to be sorted out.

Via Grace, we can lean into Life's hopeful anthem that our communities can become places of peace and growth. We may learn to own up, speak and even act on behalf of others, creating a more just economy where every person matters.

Grace is that illuminating gift that softens us and strengthens us to do the hard stuff, the tenacious offering of hope, and the intervention that protects us from going down a path that is not meant for us.

Surely Grace has been present in your life.

Love, the foundation

When I was in seminary, I went through a severe season of doubt. The movie Schindler's List played and watching it made me recoil from a God who seemed not to care about the horrific suffering and perverse conditions of men. My plans to hand over my life into the hands of God felt too risky and untenable. Not only so, suffering like this made life feel so random and pointless.

As is my habit to come clean with God, I took my case up with him. He was on the dock. Thankfully God did not retaliate. Instead, I understand now that He kindly hosted me to a special encounter with him.

To give him a fair chance to rebut, I read from the book of Romans in the Bible to reacquaint myself with what the faith was about. Then, still unable to focus on my studies, I wandered the library and a tiny book from a shelf caught my eye. It was a slim volume of meditations on the Cross, not a book I would typically read.

While my head was jammed with objections and my heart filled with fear and dread about my future, the words from the book and the Bible settled me into a new space, and I heard a question posed to me: how big is your God Jenni?

God did not chide my audacity or belittle my faith but challenged me to reimagine who He is.

Perhaps my idea of a god who is confined to the church is too small. Since God is the source of life, he must be active in the affairs of men in ways I have never considered before. It is fascinating that no matter what our creed, it is a universal manifesto of our kind that we refuse to bow to the darkness, and we deserve the light. Often, we also actively object to sufferings we witness and may work sacrificially to alleviate and remove it.

Where does this refusal and resolve arise from? What soil has allowed these vulnerable seeds of hope to continue to grow? What is this ground of being that unites us across time, culture, and circumstances?

It is the foundation of love. It lies beneath every single 'living-ness'.

The Christian faith speaks of this love not as an affection, although that is a dimension of it, but as something far deeper, greater, and eternal.

God is love (1 John 4:8)

When we track the story handed to us in the Bible, we see this Love creating, seeking, saving, restoring, judging, persisting. Love, not cupid, is waiting to spring up despite the damage, destruction, and despair many of us are familiar with.

Created out of love and in love, we are inherently wired to understand the language of love. Our bodies, minds, hearts, and souls thrive when we experience it. In fact, the ultimate suffering in our lives and in our world is this: being removed from the foundation of our well-being. Our alienation from God cuts us off from what nourishes, stabilizes and supplies us with everything we need to live sensibly and strong. We cannot think, organize, or therapize our way out of this state.

Yet God who is the Source of life keeps sending out the nourishment we need. Love flows towards us in myriad ways each day. Each unique sunrise and sunset, framed in glorious brightness and hues, are invitations to us to taste and relish the gifts of life. It beckons us to begin again and reminds us to wind down and rest. All nature calls out to us to wonder at her gifts of liveliness and her valiant fight against disease and destruction.

****

Viktor Frankl, holocaust survivor and psychiatrist described the impact of nature on the men in his book Man's Search for Meaning:

> "If someone had seen our faces on the journey... as we beheld the mountains of Salzburg with their summits flowing in the sunset, through the little barred windows of the prison carriage, he would never have believed those

faces were the faces of men who had given up all hope
of life and liberty... we were carried by nature's beauty."

This account shows the raw power of beauty to transport us
above and beyond our circumstances, to lift our spirits.

Even as we witness so much gone wrong in our world, it's
as if life itself fights back. The hashtag #faithinhumanityrestored
signals our longing to believe in something intrinsically oriented
towards life and goodness. From the kindness of a stranger to the
stirrings in our soul, we are urged to stick around and strain towards a better day.

Could these be signposts from God, inviting us to reconnect
to the foundation of life, His hospitable love?

What's more, God's desire is to draw us back to an unbro-
ken relationship with him marked by joyful trust. This is why the
Christian take on life contains at its heart a personal story, set in
human history, where this love became enfleshed. Jesus Christ,
God in the flesh, makes it easier for us to envision God's love and
respond to it. This story leads us to a small dusty hill where a Cross
stood and Christ died, in agony and in complete innocence.

This God-man had said things like -

> "I have come so that they may have life and have it in
> abundance." (John 10:10)

> "Consider the birds of the sky: They don't sow or reap or
> gather into barns, yet your heavenly Father feeds them.
> Aren't you worth more than they? Can any of you add one
> moment to his life span by worrying? (Matthew 6:26)

> "Come to me, all of you who are weary and burdened, and
> I will give you rest." (Matthew 11:28)

> "I am the way, the truth, and the life. No one comes to the
> Father except through me." (John 14:6)

In these words, God points us away from the mindset of scarcity, deprivation, and insecurity, to look out for His love found in
the goodness of pulsing life rather than be mired by our limited
horizons.

This transformation is not experienced by our grit and positivity. It required Jesus to walk the whole way to the Cross, be subject to the cruel darkness of the worst of the human heart and die under its power. But three days later, Jesus arose from the clutches of death and breaks open a new and living way for the world.

Like the old tales of treasure seeking, this new way is discovered as we follow the clues and read these hints which lead to the spot marked 'X', where we find a never-ending Spring in the shape of a cross.

The Cross conveys the love of God specifically, clearly and finally.

God calls us to release and rest, admitting that our burdens are too great and our strength too small. God shows us through Christ that there is a different way to live. But He doesn't stop there either.

We may have said a prayer, gone to church and been involved in many activities and still not found our way to the Cross such that we can exchange our hardened ways for his. So, God goes beyond to continually host us through His Grace and Love to this different way of doing life—yes, God patiently and personally nudges onward to this place of exchange where we learn to habitually relinquish our ways, lay down our guard of self-protection and defense, and pay attention to God's ways. This is where we begin to feel safe, grow sound and embrace service to others as a joyful thing.

Eight springs of Grace and Love

God, the Host of all our lives, offers the most war-worn ones of us gifts and opportunities to encounter His love and grace. I have found eight ways these have flowed, even in the most hardened of places. In both my experience and those of others I have been privileged to know, it remains true that when we open our hearts to love and grace, we will be watered, nourished and healed.

1. Encouragement

   Small things can add courage to our faint hearts to help us move forward. It could be the smile of a shy child when our eyes meet, sunshine, another coin just as we needed it, a text message from someone who cares, a warm meal, a sense of wellness and a stirring of hope.

2. Gentle Wisdom

   Not knowing what to do is a common human predicament, as is feeling overwhelmed. At such times, we may sense a wee light in the midst that gives us the clarity and even gumption to know where to plant our next step.

3. Kindness

   While most of us think of God as punitive since our ideas of authority tend to be so, He prefers to lead us by cords of kindness. When we receive kindness, we feel safer. Our needs are validated, and our worth is restored.

4. Second Chances

   There is no way to avoid mistakes and even failures. A second chance may be trying the same thing a new way or adopting a different priority that is more in line with who we are and the season of life we are in. Every transition of life in fact affords us a pause and an opportunity to choose afresh to dedicate ourselves to the gift of our life. A poor student can become a strong worker. A nonchalant child grows up and decides to be a devoted parent. A callous soul turns around and shows up with fierce dedication.

5. New appetites and tastes

Our habits form us as well as trap us. It is easy to become reliant on what we are used to and feel insecure when we cannot have what we are used to. But God knows this is a flimsy set up. Through a need to change because of life's circumstances, love and grace are offering us a chance to be free of those habits that trap us. Many new parents who embrace the sacrifices of parenthood marvel at their own growth and enlarged capacities, from delaying personal gratification to discovering the joys of children's books. This isn't primarily about food, but about values and the ways we see God, others and even ourselves. It is about receiving a fresh appreciation and having our senses reignited, thus becoming more alive and attentive to life itself.

6. Timeliness

Instead of feeling behind time, losing time or trying to catch up with it, Grace settles us into a different relationship with time. It is elusive to control the relentless march of time. Wellness and strength come when we watch for a sense of timeliness instead—what is the appointed time for things in our life. This alertness frees us from comparing ourselves with others and mimicking them, to boldly live in sync with our bodies, minds and souls.

7. Firm Instructions

Life thrives within boundaries, and Grace will issue us orders to stay or risk the consequences of trespassing. To feel a 'no' in our spirit is Grace's protective mechanism to help us stay safe. To sense a 'go' is Grace's prodding to be brave and to dare greatly in our own way. Jesus describes those who have a vital relationship with Him as being able to hear these personal instructions from Him[3]—how amazing is this!

8. Gratitude

Even the most hardened of us will have moments when we know it's only right to be thankful. This reflex points towards our nature as beings who are dependent and connected to others. It is interesting that many counsellors and therapists recommend that their clients keep a gratitude journal. Noting and expressing gratitude is a key way towards mental and emotional wellness. To be grateful is to acknowledge that we are recipients. It is to direct thanks towards a giver, and God silently accepts it as He continues to order His flow of grace and love towards us.

We come upon all of these in serendipitous ways via nature, other people, changes in weather and circumstances, shifts in our own soul and mind, and reversals in life circumstances. Grace is neither wishful thinking nor sentimentality. It is God's hospitality toward us. When it comes, it seeks to be welcomed by us, so that it can enter our being, and we discover the true nature of life.

As a pastor I have witnessed many who have shut the door to grace, and it is heartbreaking. I think of a man who had an amazing tenacity but kept plodding in a direction that only caused hurt to all those around him. Riddled by childhood traumas, he had only one mode and speed: fast and furious. As I thought about him and the ways different ones have appeared to help, I see a clear story of Love and Grace at work. Even the four wives he had seemed to each present him with a gift he needed sorely. His first wife was a homely person who offered him stability. The second was a broken soul struggling with addiction who called him to seek healing with her. The third wife could have taught him to be organized and principled. Finally, the last wife was a simple, contented woman. In each instance, he remained blinded by his way of doing life, never

3. John 10:4.

received the love and grace offered and continued to live by strife, struggling and relying on his lost and limited self.

Interestingly, as we develop more sensitivity and receptivity to this flow of God's Love and Grace, we will shift from being a guest to become a host of this flow, and we get to decide if it flows onwards—more of this in part six. For now, let's slow down and recount the chapter, take time to reflect, and enjoy another beautiful poem.

Part 3 Highlights

- The world is designed to thrive as it is watered by Grace and Love, the twin characteristics of God's gracious hospitality.

- Grace does three things: it illuminates and sheds light that softens and strengthens us, it tenaciously points us towards hope, and it intervenes to protect us.

- Love is the solid presence and activity of God that pursues us towards wholeness and reconciliation with Him and others.

- Jesus Christ's words, His life, His death and resurrection are a concrete demonstration of God's love and the way God wants us to do life.

- There are at least eight ways we can receive and share these gifts of grace and love.

Soak & Savor

- Think over your life and recount instances where you received grace and love. What effect did those experiences have on you? Did the effect last, why or why not?

- Of the eight ways that God may be hosting us in grace and love, which ones have you witnessed in your own life or in others?

- This part ends with an enigmatic description that when we become a grateful guest, we can also become a host for what we receive. Sit with this thought and journal your insights.

from a place called Love

~ Nicole

I go out but I return
to a place called Love
where my roots sink deep
and the ascent is steep
where I keep the parts
of myself still broken
but now each muscle
woken each wound
a token of all that has
is unsaid
is unfelt
is undone
I used to run at the first
sight of smoke
I used to inspect the
brickwork of my gate
now it swings wide open
a field of roughness
of wild abandon
of sharp edges
of grounded earth
each breath now births
a new pair of eyes
a new heart that dies
here there are no lies
only necessary goodbyes
to the past selves that

left behind empty shells
welding the feeling to
the meaning of
suffering well and for
open windows and open doors
returning again to
the place that still remains
that calls Love by name.

"Home is the place where you are most thoroughly yourself, with no pretences."

~ VICTOR MORAN, CREATING A CHARMED LIFE

PART 4

How God's Hospitality Transforms Us

"What does a guest want?"

"... a guest wants first of all to be diverted, to get out of his daily monotony or worry. Secondly the decent guest wants to shine, to expand himself and impress his own personality upon his surroundings. And thirdly, perhaps he wants to find some justification for his existence altogether..."

THE ROADS AROUND PISA,
SEVEN GOTHIC TALES BY ISAK DINESEN

True hospitality carries power to transform. When God hosts us, He wants to move us towards His desire for us to be full and free.

Two decades ago, three small words dropped into my heart: 'Safe', 'Sound', and 'Sent'. It felt to me then that this may be what God wants for us all, to be well and live with purpose. But so much of our experiences feel far from these states. Trauma, trials and turbulence make us feel unsafe. Our buzzy and tired brains rarely afford us full confidence about our thoughts and decisions. Our hardwired and trained reflexes often launch us into frenzied activity without adequate reflection on the 'whys', leading us to exhaust ourselves.

This means that feeling safe, becoming sound and living with a sense of calling won't be up to us to construct or contrive. It feels counter-intuitive but what is required of us is to yield—so that a process of transformation may occur from the inside out.

God desires to see us shine in our full humanity and uniqueness. He knows that this will require us to experience welcome that helps us feel accepted. He offers us his life-giving presence and a sense of safety. He also challenges our beliefs and reflexes, so that we can have better tools to assess and make sense of our lives. Out of this soil of security and conviction, we are then ready to grow into our genuine and useful selves.

The question is: will we yield to being hosted by God?

1. Feeling Safe

When my daughter was old enough, I would take her for walks and to the playground. Due to my back injury, I usually needed to sit on a bench. She was curious and wanted to explore but often hesitated. She would take tentative steps before rushing back for reassurance or glance back at me to make sure that I was still on the bench. It was my steady presence which anchored her and allowed her to explore and venture further. Soon, she radiated outwards in ever-enlarging circles, her confidence growing along with it.

It dawned on me that this is much like us. We want to explore life, attempt things and develop new abilities in each season of our lives. But often enough, we may turn a corner, and the terrain would seem foreign and even dangerous. It may be a job loss, a health crisis, or the loss of a loved one. It may be hostility, betrayal, or changes because of personal convictions. All these remove the safety we once felt and can undermine our confidence. We need a parent on the bench we can run back to for orientation and assurance. Someone who can let us know we will be alright.

This intrinsic need to venture and grow is often contradicted by the fears we develop through life. These fears will keep us small and limit us as we choose to play it 'safe'.

Until we feel safe enough, it will be hard for us to explore what our lives are truly about. We would continue to live by the standards and expectations set by others, or by inner compulsions developed from trauma and our bent towards avoiding God and relying on ourselves instead. We mistake our grinding and hustling with purposeful living. This is often accompanied by haste, weariness, and a lingering sense of frustration.

With all of us struggling this way, it is little wonder that our homes and hearts are often filled with hurt and wounding. Words and actions often tumble forth before we can process them or learn to use them with loving intentionality. As a result, mistrust is high in our lives and our world. It is hard to trust ourselves and others.

The modern world we live in abets and deepens this crisis for us. As children of the knowledge economy and the internet era, turning to a search engine like Google and using AI has become a trained reflex for us.

This level of efficient haste can undermine our own thought processes and confidence in our own assessments. As a pastor, I meet highly educated folks who display a glaring lack of confidence to deal with decisions and certain aspects of life.

The lack of safety and confidence is made worse by the widespread distrust that is gnawing at all of us as we take a different view of things, hold to different values and espouse different ideals. Our brains, seeking consonance, conspire to subscribe to confirmation bias and we practice selective listening with finesse. We also find it hard to know who to trust while we live with crises looming large, with contrarian voices predicting both doom and deliverance.

Distrust is extremely toxic as it presumes the other is 'guilty' and lays down an *a priori* verdict. Sadly, this is the approach today. We pick up the newspapers expecting to find news that we will object to. We engage with social media to like, dislike or opine based on the most superficial understanding of any situation. We half-listen to one another, more focused on how we will respond to trump the conversation. As a result, many of our relationships are strained, dysfunctional and eventually break down.

My pastoral counsel has been sought for all kinds of relational wreckage, from close friendships that are torn asunder, to siblings quarrelling past their parents' demise, to crises in marriage and parenting.

The frenetic pace of city living doesn't help: so much is going on and pursued that there is little space and time for careful thought and genuine exchange. Our lives seem to be ruled by the ticking clock and the flush of unending activities.

Another reason lies in how self-actualization is pursued today. Whereas personal identity and purpose used to be woven out of a web of relational obligations, today, in seeking self-realization, the reference point narrows down to The Self, a small space which cannot afford us the deep stability we need. While seeking to assert our identity confidently, we struggle with whether anyone really wants or needs us.

In the face of all these, how can we possibly feel safe enough to explore our lives and what we aspire for them to be? Furthermore, as the joke goes. 'God loves you, and everybody has a wonderful plan for your life', means that others often have plans and expectations which at times can end up putting us in a straitjacket. Thus, safety isn't something we feel readily so we often act or react out of fear.

God seeks to graciously host us to this sense of safety.

He can do it by invitation or by intervention. Through either or both ways, God desires that we come to him simply as we are, without the need to pretend or impress. Allowing us to just be, he nudges us towards an honest look inward to admit that we are both mysterious and messy. If we would slow down and gaze upon our lives, even the wounds would begin to bear the truth that God's love and grace remains real and present.

I was excited when the church committee called me to discuss my plans after seminary. I had already shared that I sensed a call to become a pastor. Sadly, I was flatly told at the meeting that my church needed a male pastor who was married with children. This is an understandable need and a usual template most churches use in the personnel search. But I came away saddened at how my personhood and calling was not the focus of the conversation. They had, after all, affirmed me and were supporting me through seminary. Now that I am wiser and older, I know there are many other dynamics at play, but the experience showed me how easy it is for us to look past a living person and reduce them to a task or a statistic, and how that can hurt. It would have been easy for me to react in dismay and stress over my work prospect.

While the church could not offer me the safety of acceptance and a job, God did. He set me up with a church that allowed me to express my vocation and hone my skills. The excitement soon overtook any loss I felt. In time, this experience also carved within my being a compassion for others struggling to live, work and contribute to our world.

We do not need to tire ourselves through treadmill mantras of self-validation or a hungry search for the approval of others.

Instead, we can run back as often as we need to the bench where God is always ready to embrace us with soothing comfort and truthful salve. He will listen to us babble about what we found surprising, scary or what has scarred us.

With my tear-stained Bible and journal, I realized over time that praying was about sharing my heart's cry with the one who formed my heart. The hard ground, watered by tears, softened to reveal tiny springs of life. There was an artesian spring that continuously watered my life, rooting my identity beyond my needs, wants, lack and losses. Over time, I felt a strange confidence rising within me, and my voice and God's comingled to tell me that I am safe. I felt seen and known, accepted and belonged. A surge of invincibility coursed through my being and the trails and trials of life ahead seemed to take on the correct proportions. The fear of loss and uncertainty was slowly replaced by comfort and a sense of confidence that allowed me to be at peace with my story, and thus to venture forth again.

God's hospitality when I felt lost and forlorn, disoriented and in distress, rescued me from despair, cynicism and falling prey to the wolves of fear. He is my safe person and safe place as I felt His unconditional welcome, a gentle pull to cease from striving and just be. In His love for me, He also refused to let me wallow or shirk from who He made me to be by issuing me challenges that helped me forge ahead to really live. These challenges helped me to grow sound and embrace a sense of purpose afresh.

2. Becoming Sound

It may seem impossible for humans to agree or experience unity. Amid such a setting in the early church, with groups comparing and in conflict, the apostle Paul's letter addressing this situation included these enigmatic words:

> The person with the Spirit makes judgments about all things, but such a person is not subject to merely human judgments, for, "Who has known the mind of the Lord so as to instruct him?"
> But we have the mind of Christ. (1 Corinthians 2:15)

He appeals to a startling truth: those who call themselves followers of Christ have been given a new capacity to think like Christ. Setting aside our skepticism, this holds out incredible hope for us. It is possible, as each of us matures, that we can grow towards oneness as we discard our old habits of suspicion and strife.

Of course, Christ's mind is far from a dull, one-track organ, and we ought not to take this to mean that we will all think alike. The gift of this capacity will interact with everything that is given and grown in our heads and hearts. The Greek word used here refers to the use of the mind to discern and arrive at an understanding of the truth.

But much stands in the way of us becoming sound this way.

Over sixty thousand music tracks are uploaded each day and over 2.5 quintillion bytes ply the internet highways daily. Each of our brains as adults run through an average of 60000 thoughts each day, which intersect and collide with the music and bytes around us.

Thinking a thought slowly and thoroughly seems a strange and untenable proposition these days, with the swift bombardment of information and our all-too-easy dependence on sound bites. Being rightly informed and making strong decisions is increasingly difficult.

The Greek word for the sound mind, *sophroneo*, is a compound word combining *sodzo* and *phroneo*. *Sodzo* means to be saved or delivered, while *phroneo* is the use of the mind. A sound mind is one that is rightly used, saved from distortions and disarray. In terms of our identity and purpose, becoming sound is the experience of having one's storyline moored to something stable, such that the thinking that issues forth is a consonant plotline despite the inevitable twists and turns. In the process of examining our thoughts, soundness grows as it is anchored and re-anchored from the ravages of lies, half-truths, and contradictions that work against it. The Bible refers to this as a renewing of our mind.

To renew something is to be in possession of it first. God grants His children the capacity to think differently and beyond the material information available. In Colossians, we are told that this must be revisited faithfully-

> "... put on the new self who is being renewed to a true knowledge according to the image of the One who created him.." (Colossians 3:10)

This Scripture tells us that our true sense of self is a process of discovery that grows along with our knowledge of God. We must endeavour to establish our self-knowledge according to the truth that we are being conformed to be like Christ. Yet most of us focus on how far we are from being like Christ and often become cowered by the fears that stalk us. These fears are at the heart of the narrative we weave about who we are.

Both psychology and neuroscience show us how important and powerful personal stories are, especially our origin stories. They set the stage for our lives, and though we may take many turns and even turn away from them, we can never be completely free of them. Indeed, the lodging for our identity, worth, vocation is our personal story, and it is often filled with imperfections that hurt us deeply. No wonder that we find our accommodation limiting and perhaps even unwelcome. It is not easy to be at peace with ourselves.

Perhaps to manage and cope, the modern self is now malleable and infinite, completely defined by a radical individualism. This seems to offer a sense of freedom and empowerment. But the constant need to self-define, protect and project is an onerous and wearisome undertaking.

By contrast, the Christian metanarrative situates each of our lives, as diverse as the billions of us there are, within an origin story that can hold our personal stories as well as allow us to interact with others' stories and journeys without threat. This requires us to admit and risk the need to go beyond the story arc we feel we can manage to enter a larger story—God's story.

The story of Creation in the Bible speaks of goodness, abundance, jubilation, and hospitality. God created the conditions that would allow humans to live, work and thrive. Yet, the story goes awry as the first pair responded to an enticement and acted out a good instinct for growth and preservation by leaning away from faith.

Even then, the story upon closer inspection reveals a tender God who continues to offer hospitality. Having to limit the pair's access, God tenderly sacrifices from his creation to sew together the first garments to protect the pair from the elements.

The male and female pair received from God, whose image they were made in, the firm word of a father as well as the sheltering care of a mother. They may have let God down, sinned and broken the way the world was meant to run, but they remain ever under the watchful eye of the parent.

The rest of the Bible is filled with history, story and poetry about God's Love that wants to unite humankind back to himself.

To illustrate this, the Bible unlike many other religious texts, detail the story of a group of people whom God elected. The people of Israel were slaves, but they would become free, with a sense of identity, morality and purpose. The descriptors for them were astounding to say the least, including being "my people", "a priesthood", "light to the nations". God desires a similar narrative for our lives too—to be set free and discover our potential and promise.

Alas the bent of man towards self-sufficiency and wantonness meant that they largely failed. Yet there remained a scarlet thread of redemption running through individuals, families and even time periods where the story of life is one of peace, stability, and possibility.

This thread would wend its way to a cruel cross during the great Roman Empire, where human hubris and evil were phenomenal. Into this realm and way of things, Jesus Christ spoke and worked truth, setting the story of life against the story of empire and religion. His death which seemed a defeat ushered in a new era for humanity.

When we read this grand movement in human history, where God is persistently hosting us toward life, our usual storylines which are largely about avoiding pain and death can now be rewritten: there is another way to live where we do not have to be the author, editor, and publisher of our lives.

Instead, we take on a journalistic curiosity to figure out the true meaning of our lives and the lives of others. We don't have to engineer, control, or manipulate every plot development as it rests on a larger narrative that is being held and developed by God. Rather, we learn to decipher if we are following a narrative script that we were handed, one we generated ourselves out of fear and strife, or one that rings true based on faith and trust.

As a woman of faith and vocation, and married to a fellow pastor, expectations from others and myself can blanket me with the suffocating need to prove myself and to live a glaringly positive story for others. This would only create a persona and trap me in the way of strife. If I relied on the usual ways of survival by trying harder, my issues may go underground. Instead, I see now on hindsight how my mind grew sound as my story line became clearer through my habits of prayer and feeding on the revelation in God's Word.

2. Becoming Sound

My daily times of prayer were not so much about the strength of my faith or faithfulness, but that each day God was available for me to go to Him with my bundles and bumbling. Repeatedly, God enabled me to detach from what would stifle and even misshapen who I am as I was able to feel safe to bear my doubts, hurts and aspirations. Patiently, like the tedious work of sorting beans, I felt God worked with me to distinguish the shadows from the substance. This process of renewing and anchoring my mind resonates with Jesus' word[1] to us that we are to be sound and clear, letting our Yes and our No be distinct. This is soundness—it develops definition, hones fidelity, grows courage and develops a way of speaking that brings clarity.

---

1. Matthew 5:37.

3. Being Sent

God's hospitality, the love that heals, restores, grows, and solidifies us, also sends us forth into the world. To taste the loving hospitality of God is to share it with others.

The early Christians were clear headed about this. Understanding life as a gift and God as the host, they exemplified this by taking in abandoned babies and children, elevating the status of women and welcoming slaves as brothers and sisters in the faith. This was in complete opposition to the values of the day which were marked by decadence and oppression. For this they were both admired, with many joining their ranks and being vilified to the point of martyrdom. This paradoxical response is what every Christian must come to expect as persons and communities that are called to join God in his love and grace.

Jesus described the Christian faith not in terms of holding on to exactingly accurate ideas of God, but as an ongoing, daily choice to yield to God's higher, perfect way of love:

> "If anyone wants to follow after me, let him deny himself,
> take up his cross daily, and follow me." (Luke 9:23)

What I did not expect was how this yielding led to the back alleys and forgotten neighborhoods of my life. There are things we would rather forget, places we may not want to revisit and memories we refuse to recount. But these have all been a part of our becoming and precisely because they are unwelcome, they become feed for the wolves. Often, naming, reclaiming and reframing them are necessary.

I had to confront them when I worked on the timeline of my life. Another time, a suppressed memory returned to me. Then my dreams woke me to hidden fears and anxieties.

While we should certainly not try to exorcise demons that may not exist or reach back into our past without guidance, God can and does stay with us as the unperturbed Host and offer us salve for our wounds and shield us from the howling winds that blow in the caverns of our souls.

Most of us would prefer not just Instructions for Life, but also the Wand of Makeover. The latter is what we want God to do, to undo all the damage others have done to us and we have done to ourselves and others. This is the false notion of a fresh start. Nothing changes when our circuitry remains the same.

Something deeper, more surgical, and entirely radical must happen. But we could not bear it without the anesthetic touch of God's Love.

Even as we develop strategies to preserve and protect ourselves from hurt, each episode is like shattered glass, too painful to pick up. It is only the patient and persistent love and grace of God and his unfailing kindness and tenderness that would smoothen the jagged and sharp edges of suffering and loss so that I could begin to hold and handle them. I picked up each piece, from deprivation in childhood, sexual assaults, and misogynistic treatment received, to name how they have hurt me, and refuse their hold over my life. As I did this, the wolves slowly slink away, now that they do not sense me as an easy prey.

As God granted me the safety and soundness to encounter and process any past sin, wounds and difficult memories of my past, He taught me how to move ahead and wield the light well. His call to us to be salt and light is not to impose our well-meaning agendas on others, but to bear witness to the grand love and grace we have come to know as real.

In following Jesus, I would have to face myself, and deny the self that wants to wrench control, run from pain and avoid the truth. I would have to die to my tendencies to take the softer option, sidestep issues and fail to truly see or hear another person. I would have to feel the weariness of cross bearing for the growth of self and for the wellness of others.

Whereas in my youthful zeal, I spent long days and nights perfecting programs and executing tasks, I now see that God was sending me to mimic what He does for me—create space, foster authenticity and empower.

I began to learn to observe the contours of the human *soulscape*, what lurks there and how God wants to turn every wasteland into a garden. Compassion began to grow within me, and I found a new ability to sit with those who suffer, not demand that they heal, yet point them towards hope.

By all counts from his record on earth, Jesus loved being with the marginal and disenfranchised. This means that you can simply show up. You no longer must lug around the dead weight of the parts you may have marginalized in yourself. Jesus will welcome and embrace you just as you are. Then he will love you towards the courage to discover your loveliness. He will help you pick up the fragments of your life and face them. As you stay on track, you will begin to see that an astonishing mosaic is coming together.

Following this Saviour will always take you outward from a place of inner work to serve others. It does not require grand gestures though. Many problems in life do not go away easily and most of us lack the wisdom to bring any 'solutions' if they are even possible. But we can do the one thing no system, protocol or plan will ever suffice: be present.

Humans are relational beings, and we find our sense of self and well-being in relationships where we feel wanted, belonged and valued. Whether it is a pet, a therapist, or an old friend, the presence of others is essential. Introvert or extrovert, we all need another living soul we can relate to in a meaningful way.

Mother Teresa famously said that the worst disease for mankind is loneliness. In her work of offering presence to the dying, who due to their disease and the impoverished realities are often left abandoned, she restores their human dignity when she goes to them and offers them the safety and salve to leave this earth in dignity.

Can we imagine a world where we turn toward one another and learn to be together, without the need to fix one another? Can we admit, through simple kindness, that suffering is a part of living? Can we shift from seeing joy and pain as opposites and allow them to co-exist in us and among us?

Jesus bore the weight of the world, and he laughed. He went to a wedding, knowing the wine would run out, and compassionately made more. He never told anything but hard truths and used everyday stories to convey them. He showed us how to live - brave and honest.

He then goes on to make this way of life possible by dealing with the heart of the issue: our hardwired way of grasping and seeking control—the hellish bent to be independent of God, to be gods ourselves. Through his death and resurrection, Jesus offers us a new and living way.

This new way takes time to acquaint and accept.

We are creatures of habit and reflexes. In my journey I found I had much to unlearn, let go of, and yield. This journey would be a hard Sisyphean slog if it were all up to us. But to be hosted by God, watching him provide, guide, listen, comfort, and exhort, charged the journey with a glory and beauty that transfigured me and the way I live.

This means that whether it is a conversation with my spouse, a work meeting or a large conference, I am not in charge. God is, and I am to trust his flow of love and grace and co-operate with it. This has dramatically changed my posture, tone and expectations.

The most immediate effect of this transformation is felt in my closest relationships. In times of stress and conflict, I imagine God being present as the host and it tampered my responses. I certainly behave better when God is in the room. I realized that I no longer had to fight to have the last word in a vain effort to control the outcomes. As I learnt to loosen my grip, my marriage and family life had more room to flourish. I also found my attitude towards work shift. I embrace the Sabbath as I began to understand the limits and boundaries required for me to grow in wholeness and bring my best self. As God hosted me, His love and grace filled my being. I continued to feel safe and sound in my knowledge that every engagement and interaction was a missional moment, where God is present and seeking to host all to wholeness and fullness.

Humans are transcendent beings with a longing for purpose, meaning and significance. We can seek these on our own or return to God and allow Him to send us forth, where we rest in his hospitality and partner it as he entrusts us with the opportunities and resources. Every moment of our lives can become a means through which we develop a greater consciousness of God's love and grace, taking our focus away from our own limited and self-centered assessments of the situation.

This is an adventure of growth and as the below passage puts it, it can include difficult terrain. But notice how intimate this journey is, where God's whispers can be counted on:

> Although the Lord gives you the bread of adversity and the water of affliction, your teachers will be hidden no more; with your own eyes you will see them. Whether you turn to the right or to the left, your ears will hear a voice behind you, saying, "This is the way; walk in it." (Isaiah 30:19–21)

Part 4 Highlights

- The change and transformation of our lives is an act of God.

- He makes this possible by giving us a new life when we hand our lives over to Him, trusting that Christ has bridged us back to a vital father-child relationship with God.

- God alone can restore the safety, soundness and purpose of our lives.

- The fuller story of our experiences emerges, and we flourish as we trust Him to host us towards outcomes of wholeness and fullness.

Soak & Savor

- Free your imagination and describe what this may be like for you:
  - » Feeling safe
  - » Becoming sound
  - » Being sent

- Consider what transformation God may be hosting you towards?

- What may help you to yield to God's transforming grace and love?

- Which of the three transformative outcomes from God's grace and love call out to you/?

- How may you go about receiving this experience?

The Busker's Psalm

~ Eric Valles

Hear the cover singer paint golds and blues
in the quest for a perfect tune.

Banging a portable keyboard, he bellows in the dark;
his calling's to croak like the best on a sidewalk;
his head in a daze, heart yearning for the sun,
he builds a ladder to touch an LCD screen sky.

The minstrel drops a new cover in every season,
syncopated rhythms in frenzied time
slashing the air until the cold sets in
on his cot on an imagined pinewood stage.

Misplaced notes, uninspired verses
do not stop this thrush from opening its beak.
Neither hearts of stone nor ears of concrete
make him stray from the nest he seeks.

A knock on his flat's door, like tympani in a dream,
suspends his tour with a debt collector's screams.
A brown-frocked choir chants his worldly name
and raises him up to a light-drenched banquet hall.

Hear cover singers paint golds and blues
in our quest for the perfect tune.

"Home isn't where you're from.
It's where you find light when all goes dark"

~ PIERCE BROWN, GOLDEN SUN

PART 5

Let God Host You

Being hosted requires that we adopt a fundamental change in orientation and posture. We must be willing to receive. It is interesting how many of us struggle to receive as it feels to us like weakness. We love being in control.

But our control is at best an illusion. If God designed life to operate by grace, we must relinquish being in charge and instead retrain ourselves to be more willing to live as recipients. Thankfully, this process is undergirded by God's grace and love too.

I found that there are seven spaces that can help us restore and cultivate our creaturely and childlike dependence on God.

These spaces help us recognize how life flourishes when we worry less about its fragility but choose instead to celebrate its fecundity. When we loosen our grip on things and relationships, they will have more breathing space and time to develop and mature.

In fact, when we think about how we are all guests at God's table, and how that can transform us, we can live lighter and approach every interaction with gratitude and openness. This holds the potential for conflicts to deescalate, for voices to be heard, and for resources to be pooled.

To enter these spaces, we must whet our appetite.

Savor

Consider these words from God Almighty in the Psalms:

> O taste and see that the Lord is good;
> How blessed is the man who takes refuge in Him! (Psalm 34:8)

We are invited to approach God with the expectation that we can savor Him. It might feel odd to imagine God as something we can take in. We are urged to partake of who God is, letting Him enter the depths of our being, digesting it so that God is infused within. In a sense, His grace and love become the building blocks of our lives the way amino acids, lipids and nucleotides work to form our biological being.

This is no mere religion. It is more accurate to call it a union.

The Scripture describes tasting God's goodness occurring as we take refuge in Him.

The despondent and losers in warfare in ancient times as to-day often seek refuge in caves or places of deprivation, an experience that reinforces their lowly status and sense of defeat. It is not the same with God. As we seek refuge from Him, His stature and strength will not overpower us. Instead, it gradually leads us to a state of blessedness as all of God's goodness fills us bit by bit.

The needs of our lives and of the world do not escape God's loving attention.

Once we strip away our faulty notions of hospitality, and recognize life is a gift offered to us by God the Host, our approach to life will be radically altered. We can awaken our senses to consider where God's goodness might be present to us. We can join others who are further along with their experience and welcome those who may find it foreign.

If you read this far, you may have found evidence of grace and love in your life. May I urge you to consider the seven spaces which are being described next, for God has designed these as distinct places of nourishment and encounter.

I am aware that some of these spaces, like the home and the family, are unfortunately sources of trauma and deep pain for many. But suffering, pain and death will not have the final word, for God wants to creatively redeem and re-create these places for us. We will have to risk and respond to the invitation to go get a taste. Indeed, a life of joy is not escapism but engagement where one is able to taste the deeper flavours that can only be found in the tart, bitter and harsh.

Seven Spaces

1. FAMILY

We need more than a space to live in; we need a place to belong to. All societies have a way to address this primal need. There is a need for a space in which we derive our names, find shelter and develop our sense of self.

Fascinatingly, God addresses this need. He grants all who believe in him to be known as children of God (John 1:12). When asked how we ought to pray, Jesus taught that we are to call God *Abba*, an intimate term for father in Aramaic.

The Scripture says that "he sets the lonely in families" (Psalm 68:6 NIV). One of the most powerful metaphors for the church is that it is a family or household. Jesus Himself responded to a request to come out of a crowded home to greet His mother and brothers with the reply that " whoever does the will of my Father in heaven is my brother and sister and mother." (Matthew 24:50)

Tracing the storyline, we can say that God is looking to reunite with His children, by reconstituting a family that goes beyond genes, geography, culture and history. It is the ultimate inclusiveness we intuit as most true of humanity.

Sadly, our idea and experience of the family is often fraught with pain, regret and even disdain. The modern family unit is breaking down at phenomenal rates around the world from divorce, violence, war, migration, and work. With this comes an increased sense of homelessness. Although we all have a first family and home, it is easy these days to be made orphaned and homeless, both literally and emotionally.

But with God as our Father, and His people as community, we need not be bereft. We can find a sense of home and family from those who would show us kindness, offer us help or just grant us the gift of patience as we struggle and heal.

These people are family to us, helping us find who we are once again, and what our lives are about. Their offer of time, physical or emotional assistance and other practical help can be restorative for our broken hearts. They often help connect the disparate dots of our lives to help us take the next step.

This family could be a church, communities of intention, foster homes and shelters or a kind stranger—no matter young or old. It can be for an hour or a lifetime. But what each opportunity offers is an extension of the foundational hospitable love of God that lays beneath all acts of hospitality.

2. NATURE

The climate crisis makes it clear that wanton consumption of natural resources may fatten us for a while but ultimately readies us for the slaughter in the end. We must acknowledge that we are a part of a larger circle of life and reconsider our habits. This obvious need for change will not be met with the commitment required unless we admit that we are fellow creatures with plant and animal life, and that we were given the mandate to steward this earth.

This is our origin story given to us in the Bible, and it establishes for us that God is the Host, and we are all guests who must learn to behave and get along in order to enjoy the wondrous hospitality freely offered to us.

This is captured in one of the songs in the Bible:

> *How countless are your works, Lord!*
> *In wisdom you have made them all;*
> *the earth is full of your creatures.*
> *Here is the sea, vast and wide,*
> *teeming with creatures beyond number—*
> *living things both large and small.*
> *There the ships move about,*
> *and Leviathan, which you formed to play there. (Psalm 104:24–26)*

Notice the reference to play. God has not designed life to be a set of functions, which is a serious error many of us make as we measure each other by our grades and output. The reference to play speaks of safety, order, and delight. We should head out to nature to regain our sense of awe, and walk reverently among creation, careful not to taint and destroy any of it as we do so.

As a child, I received little supervision or structure, so it's not unusual that I would sometimes wander around the neighborhood. One such time, I stopped to watch a stray cat. I was mesmerized. Here was a creature much smaller than me that had the audacity to claim a space and relax as if it owned it. Who or what gave the cat this amazing sense of self?

From that point on, every animal was a subject of curiosity and potential friendship, and who better to discuss it all with than the Creator? I talked incessantly with God about all that He made and marveled at the diversity and capacities of each one I met. I did not know it then, but nature was probably the church beyond church walls for me, where my young soul was shaped through the delight and joy of the liveliness of things.

3. LITURGY

It is good that this is a word we are learning to reclaim for our time. We are creatures of desire and habit, and liturgy is simply a set order of things that capture our imagination and draw out our desires. It is possible to use this word for what goes on in marketing and politics today, or even in seemingly mundane day-to-day living. The fast-food drive-through is designed like a liturgy to take us from one stage to the next in order to satisfy our desire for food. Liturgy is everywhere, for we are designed to respond to it.

It is no wonder that God, in helping to establish the people of faith, gave clear instructions for a physical edifice and specific acts of worship to draw their attention, fill their heads and shape their hearts.

The church liturgy, which combines music, movements, proclamation and the Eucharist where we focus afresh on Christ, was meant to help do the same. It may seem laborious to some of us, but the truth bears repeating as we forget easily and are subject to other liturgies each day.

Alas, our pragmatic bent towards efficiency has disinclined many of us as we speed through a weekend worship service. We get bored with the set prayers and repetitive feel of what is being done, forgetting that they are meant to serve as anchors for our souls and communities, delivering us from our tendencies to be enticed by novel ideas and feelings and being swept away by eddies of change.

In many more modern churches, God is sometimes reduced to the projections of our human need, rather than the true God who existed before time and called everything into existence—the One who sustains everything with a telos in mind.

A good liturgy will help us to reframe our personal narratives so that we recall the safety God provides, renew our minds towards soundness and embrace the call on our lives to serve others. It is to be reminded of the bigger story of God's love, a God that seeks to reunite with His beloved yet lost and broken world.

Going to church and engaging meaningfully isn't an optional activity when we recognize that it is a special space where God is hosting us towards becoming His beloved family. It must be an embodied experience and not something we can do online all alone by ourselves at home. As we understand that God is hosting us, we come as equals with our offering and our burdens. There in the safety of God's love and goodness, we can learn to listen to the stories of others and discover points of intersection. Such is the sublime joy of sharing in a faith community where we agree on the gems found in Scripture or good books, support each other through both the triumphs and trials of life, and find kindred souls to dream together of better days.

4. TABLE

A special part of the liturgy is the Table of Communion. This, is a space in itself to savor God's grace and love.

The meal table, on a rug on the floor or elevated on wood or stone, is a place of acceptance, belonging and sustenance. As our modern appetites and way of life often turn it into a place of control and contest (how huge a mess, who will pay and so forth), we are all longing for a conversion of our tables from mere eating place to a space for nourishment, relational deepening, and enjoyment.

This means we must desire and design our table experiences.

A model of an ideal meal table is the table of the Lord. During His final meal before His death, Jesus showed us what a table is meant to do.

As the host, he gets up and goes to every individual to wash their feet, a task usually relegated to a lowly servant. God's table calls us to settle in comfortably and not carry the dirt and mud of the world with us. It is to come apart, settle down and just be.

Jesus then reclines and enjoys the meal as he shares his heart with them. The conversation is filled with questions and authentic responses. God's table calls us to be vulnerable and honest, baring our thoughts and our soul.

Finally, Jesus breaks the bread and serves the wine. He asks His disciples to do likewise when they gather. It is important to note that Jesus did not enact the Holy Communion as a religious act but used a regular meal and imbued it with fresh meaning. Thus, it becomes the true and lasting meal we all need as it reminds us what life is truly about, and where true sustenance comes from: a restored relationship with God as we receive forgiveness and partake of Christ himself.

Many contemporary churches have lost the depth of this Eucharistic encounter as we reduce it to a set format often done in short shrift. When we recognize how powerful this act is, we should see to design one that will unite our body, heart and mind—as we bow, move slowly, receive and savor, guided by thoughtful words. It is less about a private moment with God than a corporate renewal of our shared identity. This is why we pass the peace and verbalize the words together in unison. It is a meal to gather us back to a shared center and call us to disavow our divisive tendencies.

The entire process is filled with discipline and intentionality.

Drawing from this, we can create more meaningful experiences for our daily meals too. We often hurriedly say a worn word of thanks before we tuck in, and eat hastily, without fully taking in the gift of the meal or the company we have.

All meals are a sign of the Eucharistic meal that sustains us, and we can revel in how the textures, tastes, smell, sights and sound around a table are gifts of goodness that pervades all creation and comes from Original Good.

The Bible speaks of how a banquet awaits us when we finally reunite with our Father in heaven—a lavish feast for our fullest enjoyment in diverse company, described as coming from every tribe and nation.

What if all our meals now can be a small foretaste of that?

5. WILDERNESS

This is not a space we would naturally choose but might find ourselves in. We can come to it through many routes, including loss, sickness, and brokenness.

In the wilderness, we feel disoriented and must find resources to survive. It is wild and feels harsh, but it is the precise severe mercy we need to turn inward and see what is really going on within us. The wilderness allows us to reflect on how we have viewed God and others. It is a time of deconstruction and reconstruction, where our old, tired ways and methods give way to new ways of seeing, working and even feeling.

Interestingly, the Hebrew word for the desert and the holiest part of the Tabernacle share the same root referring to a place of dialogue. Thus, it appears that inherent in these spaces is a call to slow down, examine and even wrestle so that one remains alive. It requires that we enter a deeper conversation with ourselves, and with God.

The wilderness strips us down to essentials and helps us let go of what we no longer need for our ongoing journey. We release the things that weigh us down and hinder us—from untruthful thought patterns to unrealistic dreams. As these layers that obfuscate our lives get peeled off, the self that God created in love is slowly revealed. It is time to embrace this person and not the one we have curated.

Psychologists describe our individual ways of navigating the world as schemas. My schema was to grasp at life and avoid pain because of the insecurity I felt and the tension that was often thick in my neighborhood. But our schemas are poor substitutes for what we need: salvation. The fractured self that hides and strikes out at God and others needs to be gently put back towards wholeness. It usually requires a sojourn into the wilderness, a raw and frightening place where our schemas will be glaringly inadequate.

I was not expecting huge and prolonged treks through such intimidating terrain. There was the intellectual meltdown in the face of the world's suffering, particularly the Holocaust. There were the dark nights of abject loneliness and feeling forsaken through my marriage and vocational struggles. There were the hard days of facing loss.

My sturdy edifices of self-protection and defense crumbled like a sandcastle when the fierce winds blew. Even as I could no longer hold on to them, I found that God was holding on to me. I noticed that I still live despite having no tools for survival in the desert. Indeed, many lifeforms dwell in such a seemingly inhospitable land. Clearly, my life was not in my own hands.

Slowly, I found a way to stand and move in this unfamiliar space. I was functional despite how arid and dead I felt within. Then I noticed and learned to sit with the beauty of the untamed wild, and began to embrace the gifts found in this unwelcome place:

- How the barrenness reflects my soul
- The way life can go on because the source isn't found in me
- The folly of demanding that I could only be loved if God acted in ways I could concoct
- The realization that God's love and grace works in ways that are often mysterious and require me to be receptive towards them.

With everything stripped away, the essential truth stood in stark clarity: God is the ultimate reality and ground of all being. His self-reference is that he is 'I AM"- the ever-present and all-powerful God, the only one able to sustain and nurture me in the wilderness, for no one else deigns to go there. The answer to this question is a resounding Yes:

"Can God prepare a table in the wilderness? (Psalm 78:19)

6. SCRIPTURE

The Bible is a mirror that gives those who dare to look an accurate picture. It is the water that quenches our thirst for assurance. It is a plough that breaks up the soil of our lives, revealing rubble that needs to be cleared so that seeds sown will germinate and bear fruit in time. It is a hammer that strikes the needful blow to our self-deception and hubris.

The raw power of Scripture is encountered when we go beyond mere reading and literary comprehension. All of these are experienced when Scripture is read slowly, thoughtfully and preferably in good company. The Word speaks personally as well as corporately, shaping our individual souls and bringing hearts that tend to pull away toward each other in mutual affection and humble admission of our need for each other.

My church tradition taught me well to study the Bible. But it risked reducing my relationship with God to a literary exercise or worse, to a long trudge of biblical literacy and mastery that filled my head with information and my heart with pride.

Through difficult or dry seasons, my answers and efforts kept coming up short. There are things in life that defy easy explanations. They call for us to admit that we are finite in every way. Our trust in our ability to make sense of things will be severely challenged as we experience life's breakages.

I began to understand a different way of approaching Scripture one day when I was at a retreat center. The room was empty, and I was a little listless and weary of ongoing challenges. I knew the marvelous promises in Scripture, but they felt far and unreal to me. This was because I still operated on a cognitive basis which relied on my grasping hold of what each passage meant.

The retreat leader came in and began to lead us in a slow reading of Scripture, inviting us to imagine being present at the scene. While I was at first uncomfortable, I realized it made sense to engage my entire being, including my imagination as I read and prayed. Lectio Divina, reading to hear God's voice and enter His presence was different from what I was used to. As I participated in the story, I felt much more for what was going on and surprised myself at how much I could relate to the different characters.

The experience showed me that Scripture is not a piece of religious literature to master, but more a gift of God that hosts me to encounter myself, common humanity and God himself.

I now read Scripture with a different kind of hunger, not so much to know, but to be shown that I am known and still loved. Scripture bears God's heart to us and entering the sacred pages is a time of encounter, dialogue, and transformational exchange. God hosts our humanity within those pages filled with authentic stories of human foibles, longings, and the grand story of realized hope.

7. CROSS

The cross is a symbol of eternal and enduring truth with cosmic repercussions. It is God re-laying the foundation of love that has weakened and cracked under the immense pressure of our rebellion and animosity towards Him and each other.

It opens the way for humanity to come alive again and to live in a new way. Instead of adorning it as jewelry or being satisfied with it as a physical symbol, the Cross requires us to gaze and behold its meaning until our hearts are moved to commit to a new way of doing life.

The Cross is an instrument Christ submitted Himself to and for which He calls us to bear each day. When we do, God grants us new mindsets, heart attitudes and creative responses to our personal brokenness as well as the alienation, tension and injustices of the world.

Each church and every Christian is on a journey of continual conversion into the way of the cross. We falter, at times severely. But the cross has released the power of God into the world through the giving of the Holy Spirit to all who believe. The Holy Spirit regenerates us and transforms us so that we become agents that foster life. St Hildegard uses the term 're-green' to speak of revitalizing spaces and relationships. It is a beautiful picture of things coming to life again.

One aspect of our lives that needs to experience the power of this conversion and come to life again is our imagination. My first wisdom tooth extraction was a horrible experience. With the second one, I took all measures to be sure I saw the right dentist and even asked for a general anesthetic. They denied the latter but a friend who worked at the dental center assured me that it was a routine procedure. As it turns out, I came home with a massive headache and searing pain. It was so severe that I could not find any position that would alleviate it. My brain seemed to seize up and I was unable to think as I usually did, so there was no hope of trying to recount any truths to comfort myself.

Suddenly, I thought of the Cross and the pain that Jesus felt. I sat up on my bed, closed my eyes and began to picture the Cross. As I slowly looked upon Jesus, from his head to his toes, it was as if I could relate to the pain he felt, and after a while, it dawned on me that I had entered an experience where my own pain was no longer bothering me.

As I gazed upon the broken and stripped body of Christ nailed to one of the cruelest implements of punishment known to man, sensed the ragged emotions of those close by and thought about the callous and hardened attitudes of others, my being was jolted towards an attentiveness to the harsh realities of life and the great mercy the Cross offers. Instead of being a horrifying thing, the thought of the crucifixion quietened my being.

The spiritual life requiring our rebirth by the working of God's grace lies beyond the material realm. God did not just want to save a spot in heaven for us, but to allow us to experience a quality of life, called 'eternal' from hereon. My experience of uniting with Christ through pain revealed God's presence and power to gather me into himself. There is a life that is cross-shaped which expands us upwards to God and outwards to others.

Jesus' Word to us is that cross bearing is a daily experience for all who follow Him, and there is surprising resilience to do that because He has done it for us and helps us with it now. The Cross stands as a place we can run to, its shadow offering us shade and its power giving us solace. We can look to the Cross as we await fresh hope, even in the midst of experiencing the lacerations of the world's hostility. It is the ultimate act of hospitality as God offers Himself in exchange for our freedom. We are freed from the penalty for our rebellion against Him and the power of sin's bondage.

The Cross is Jesus hosting us and our world towards healing and wellness, as we make peace with God our Source and allow it to become the shape of our lives.

Part 5 Highlights

- God invites us to experience Him.

- Savoring happens when we attend to life as a gift to relish.

- There are seven unique spaces where we can savor God's gracious hospitality, even if our reflexes may be to avoid them because they seem foreign, barren or have been places of hurt.

- The Cross is the unparalleled and unique space where we can enter a wholly different way of doing life.

Soak & Savor

- How does the invitation to savor God sit with you? Why?

- Which of these seven spaces are your familiar with, and how has reading this helped you see them differently? Which of these spaces would you like to explore?

- Revisit your understanding of the Cross. What questions and longings do you have?

- How may your imagination help you to a fresh encounter of God?

Seven Places

~ Aaron Lee

From the cradle of family where roots intertwine,
nature's hymn thrums through leaves pushing their way
into free air. Before you know it, these uncounted
days of heat and dust have woven themselves
into a liturgy for the end of day. Guided by the moss,
traverse this parched wilderness and find your way
though colours and seasons change.
See, pilgrim— a glimpse of home and its sunlit door!
Here at the table where a gracious feast is laid,
long-loved ones embrace, their faces familiar as scripture.
Here we are bound one to another, spirits kindled
by the flame of care, our love inscribed in the heart's soft gloss.
On that day you shall be free as this song written by rain,
a melody of the wandering one come home.

(dedicated to "i.m. James Pycha (Kaua'i, Hawaii")

"The character of God's hospitality frames
appropriate earthly behaviour"

~ CHRISTINE POHL

PART 6

A Call to Cohost

God invites each of us, not to religion, but to come towards him to be loved in the fullness of our being.

He wants us to see that our lives are not made of disparate, confusing and conflicting bits, but interconnected pieces of a mosaic that come together to display a magnificent masterpiece. Seeing our lives as a gift filled with immense possibilities because of God's gracious hospitality creates an entire new approach to life, including considering ourselves co-hosts with God. Afterall, each of us is also a part of a greater whole and can impact it. God longs for us to learn that life works best when we accept His gracious hospitality and join Him as co-hosts to offer hospitality to others, so that our world can heal and flourish.

Light from the End

Regardless of what we may believe about God, few of us want to end up on the wrong side of eternity.

Jesus renders a shock to our system by unravelling our commonplace ideas and fantasies about how things end. Rather than a simplistic time of reckoning, He introduces this concrete scenario:

> *For I was hungry, and you gave me something to eat, I was thirsty, and you gave me something to drink; I was a stranger, and you invited me in, naked, and you clothed me; I was sick, and you visited me, I was in prison and you came to me. (Matthew 25:35–36)*

It is striking that Jesus identifies himself as needy. The Saviour of the world is present in the needs we encounter around us. Jesus asks us to see the needs around us as invitations to encounter Him as He is present.

In His life, Jesus illustrated this solidarity by showing up in places and with company we least expect for a respectable religious leader. He does not hobnob with the powerful but befriends the impoverished, marginalized and needy. Their needs run deeper than economics, for they are often considered suspect in society. Tax collectors for example, were disdained as traitors for capitulating to the Romans and ripping off their own communities. Others carry wounds of missteps and muddled living, like the Samaritan woman Jesus took pains to meet at the well. Still others are so unfit that they are banished to the wilderness, like the demoniac who lived among tombs. [1]

---

1. Luke 18:9–11, John 4, Mark 5.

Jesus' encounters with each of these persons were never accidental. When we slow down to read and enter the stories, we find that Jesus acted like a host to each of them. At the same time however, He made himself vulnerable to their questions and demands as if He was a guest who would be impacted by their response.

This is the dialogical character of all true interactions: we can both be touched and touch others.

Furthermore, if we are honest, we would see that we have these same needs: thirst, hunger, belonging, dignity, and freedom from bondage.

By humbly acknowledging that this scenario Jesus painted isn't about our religious good-doing but a call to recognize our common humanity, we can respond in solidarity instead.

As we move towards these needs, often requiring us to go beyond our zones of comfort, we can grow in empathy, compassion, humanity, and constructive action. It is an invitation to move away from the ways of the world, where we deploy cost-benefit analysis and often do not act for fear of being taken advantage of. Christ models for us courageous vulnerability and unwavering values in the face of opposition and misunderstanding.

This end-time scene offers us light for how we are to live now. It calls us to be honest about our needs, empathize with others and act.

Becoming A Co-Host

There is a popular dictum that we cannot give what we do not have. This is only partly true. It is true that experiences can transform us and release us to be able to offer others what we have received. As we have seen, God longs to encounter us as individuals and whole societies, to taste of His hospitable goodness, so as to change the way we view life and each other.

For this to happen though, there must exist within us a divine spark that can be ignited. We do innately have something to give, but it might be deadened and dormant.

Indeed, each of us has intrinsic worth, given to us from the moment of our creation. The marvel of our life is in coming to recognize what is already inside, by the grace of creation, and learning to bring this outside. This happens as we are willing to shift to a posture of openness about life and look out for God's gracious hospitality towards us.

The disciple John understood this via eugenics. We are bound to be like our parents, and he stated that all who trust in Christ have been given the right to become children of God.[2] The earlier passage about serving Christ among the poor, marginalized and imprisoned describes God's children as expressing surprise when they were commended. To them, it was a natural expression of who they were, and their deeds were thus unself-conscious.

Our creation is, at its core, an act of generosity—God sharing his bounty. We have been created in the image of the Generous One for generosity. Our Creator's magnanimity lies at the root of

2. John 1:12.

our being, ordaining how we would flourish, by depending on His gracious hospitality and sharing it.

Flourishing is a very different experience from producing or achieving. Its organic nature speaks of delight. When we flourish, we recognize that we neither deserve nor can create much of what we have, and yet we have something to offer others. To flourish also means to be embedded in an ecosystem that values life and the conditions that enable it.

This powerful truth began percolating in the early church, leading them to form radical communities of love and acceptance. The first Christians who were deemed as a suspect sect within Judaism began to grow and encompass wider and more varied ethnic, cultural, and socio-economic groups.

In some early churches where these realities were contradicted by groups asserting superiority based on spiritual gifts and 'brand loyalty', the apostle Paul wrote firm pastoral letters to nip them in the bud. As he addressed the many specific challenges and issues, he always built his case by calling them to stand and act from the higher order principle of their new organic reality as restored creation who can live in a new way.[3] In his letter to the Galatians, Paul even rubbishes the most popular distinctions of gender, race, and status that kept people trapped in a very stratified society by positing that union with Christ is the primary identity for the Christ follower.

Contrary to the endemic human endeavor in religion to placate God with actions, St Paul insisted that the young churches anchor themselves deep in the surpassing and abounding grace of God. This grace at work would flow forth expansively and lavishly to include others.

That Christ in us and through us would welcome and even seek out the lost and needy is taught explicitly in Hebrews:

> *Do not forget to show hospitality to strangers, for by so doing some people have shown hospitality to angels without knowing it. Continue to remember those in prison as if*

---

3. This is a notable pattern in almost all of the letters Paul wrote to the early churches, where he establishes the theological foundations for right behaviours.

you were together with them in prison, and those who are
mistreated as if you yourselves were suffering. (Hebrews
13:2–3, NIV)

This is not merely a matter of doing something morally desirable or socially uplifting. The root form of the word used for 'stranger' in Greek φιλοξενίας, philoxenia, contains a self-explanatory commitment towards love.

We have all been taught stranger danger, especially as our modern world moves towards haste and anonymity. The cure for this is to sit and behold the truth that reaching out to a stranger is precisely what Christ has done for us. We were alienated, foreign, and estranged from God. Christ came to reconcile us to God, offering God's unconditional welcome, healing forgiveness and eternal love. As we turn to Christ and entrust our lives to Him, His Spirit enters our being we begin to be able to respond to His love and experience His love for others through us.

But we are like channels that are blocked with too much debris that fresh water can only trickle forth when it is meant to gush like a living stream.

The debris is collected over the course of our lives, often unknowingly.

Growing up in poverty, I never thought I had anything to offer anyone. To compensate for the sadness that I felt over not having the things others had or a quiet peaceful home, I turned to wit and mirth. This was not a conscious strategy, but God showed me it was one of many I would use over the years. In fact, in our brokenness, we are a short step away from what Frederick Buechner called self-loathing. This level of raw honesty was new to me when I first read it, having been primed, and priding myself as a reasonably successful student and even pastor.

Each time I catch sight of one of these dark shadows in the alleyways of my soul, God tenderly draws me back with grace to a place of choosing hope and resting in God's presence and patient work in my life. The words of the famous Psalm have proven true:

*Even though I walk through the darkest valley, I will fear
no evil, for you are with me; your rod and your staff, they
comfort me. (Psalm 23;4, NIV)*

Slowly God moved to clear yet more debris, and it is an ongoing project He seems very committed to!

As a pastor, it was easy to become consumed with the grind of churning out sermons, planning programs and meeting needs. We learn in counselling to beware of transference, the process where we internalize and start to over-identify with the needs of those we counsel, as this can quickly lead to emotional overload and entanglement. There is another form of transference less talked about: the Messiah complex. After all, leadership conferences love to remind us that 'the buck stops here'—right at our desk. It is no wonder that pastors are often stressed and worn out, for we have taken on God's role as the host and become over-responsible, or responsible for the wrong things.

In hosting me towards wholeness, God led me to embrace the spiritual disciplines of observing Advent and Lent, not practices my tradition taught. Those cycles of entering more deeply into what God was doing in our world turned over the soil of my soul repeatedly to reveal how shallow the roots were, where it was diseased, how vulnerable I was to despair and discouragement. My womanly cycles at times deepened the crises for me.

Experiencing the life of Christ more deeply through a careful reading of Scripture nourished me in ways that felt like I was being seated at a feast. Although hunger pangs from my longings and dashed hopes return, I knew there was a table I could sit at where my sin-stained feet were washed, my confused head anointed, and my broken heart held.

One of the words of Jesus that struck me was His description of vocation as bearing an easy yoke and a light burden. This felt contrary to most of our experiences because we have not come loose from our own schemas and stratagems for life. The position of faith is to lean into God's Word and anticipate that our experiences will be transformed.

Ways To Co-host

God longs for us to be hospitable in our conversations and interactions, whether they be private or public, in quiet service or more dramatic moments when swift action or decisions are required. This is God's way, Christ's love, and the movement of the Holy Spirit. It is the hope for our world currently.

It especially needs to happen in our homes, towards our loved ones.

Our cultural obsession with personal optimization has left many of us deeply lonely and fragile. The home is a place of great vulnerability, and it needs to be handled with tender care. It is a place where small things can make huge differences. To speak calmly, to offer help, to report for meals and even to take the trash out can be acts where we are co-hosting to make the home a welcome and safe space for each to grow.

A friend reimagined her living quarters by hosting monthly meals and even outdoor movie film sessions. Over time, the neighbors have trickled in, gotten to know each other and established new ties across gender, age, race and religion. On a hot tropical afternoon, the kitchen will be bustling with pots on the stove and something in the oven. A few friends would arrive to set up tables and chairs on the lawn. The elderly lady who lives by herself hobbles in with her walking aid, two students giggling over something also waltz in and offer to help set the tables. The neighborhood cat gingerly darts off as more arrive. Soon there will be noise, music, food, and conversation. Often there is also silence and prayer as stories tumble out. Then real needs are met as neighbors offer help with payment or getting to a medical appointment.

In offering genuine welcome and granting people space to be themselves, two of the four dimensions of hospitality are already offered and becomes the ground for the other two: rest and growth. The same needs to happen in public physical spaces. We can slow down and take the time to listen, offer a helping hand, or start small initiatives that bring people together.

Singapore is the most religiously diverse country in the world. It would be easy for suspicion and strife to mark our relationships, but many are intentional to build understanding and relationships across our differences. Another friend initiated a community library on the ground floor of her apartment block. To her delight, neighbors began to connect and contribute and the space has since grown into a hub of conversation, care and community. The library became an effervescent space of hospitality where meals were served, skills were shared and celebrations took place. Many who lived around the area and others who were drawn to it came together to welcome children, the elderly and the migrant workers.

We can also co-host on the online space where so much hurry, anger and virtue-signaling is causing us to become impatient, rude and even demonize each other. If we want our lives to matter and to flourish, we must get off any pedestal and treadmill. We must learn to recognize that we are a part of a complex ecosystem in which our posture, speech and actions can impact others for good or otherwise.

When we are touched at a primal level, we both long for and become willing to work for healthier habitations for our souls.

Each of us can attune ourselves to God's gracious hospitality and share it with others in our daily interactions. We can learn to spot Grace and her gifts of softening and illuminating us, budging us to persevere or interrupting our trajectory. We can lean deeper into Love's presence through noticing the serendipitous gifts of encouragement, wisdom, kindness, second chances, timeliness, a sense of 'rightness' about a situation, and the bubbling of gratitude.

As we continually embrace this paradigm and posture that life is sacred, we allow the truth to mature us towards safety, growth and courage. Then we become ready to co-host and help each other to really live.

The Hospitable City of God

Christianity was never meant to be a personal religious commitment alone. God in Christ announced that God's Kingdom is being inaugurated. It has been growing in both obvious and imperceptible ways for the last two millennia and will reach a final consummation one day.

Interestingly, the vision shown to apostle John which he records for us shows the city and garden coming together—a sense that God will redeem all the abilities he has given us and that life will no longer be cut short by disease and death. It is an incredible picture of flourishing and thriving, with a flow of life from The Gracious Host:

> *Then the angel showed me the river of the water of life, as clear as crystal, flowing from the throne of God and of the Lamb down the middle of the great street of the city. On each side of the river stood the tree of life, bearing twelve crops of fruit, yielding its fruit every month. And the leaves of the tree are for the healing of the nations. No longer will there be any curse. The throne of God and of the Lamb will be in the city, and his servants will serve him. (Revelation 22:1-3)*

This picture is too hard for us to grasp until we taste and attest to God's goodness and lay down our arms as we rest in the safety He grants.

Historically, hospitality has been a mark of civilization, a step up from barbarism. Welcoming someone in many cultures involves protocols where weapons are laid down first. But our cities have turned out to be brutal spaces often filled with violence towards nature and each other. The hyperconnectivity and easy access to information has created more weariness and left us restless and disconnected at deeper levels. In this light, we must wonder if we have truly progressed.

In a world unattuned to God's way and often hostile towards God, we have cut ourselves off from the ground of our being, our first original home.

To feel at home with others and work together to offer a sense of home for others require that we first experience being homed by God. This truth and feeling are easily lost to us, so we have to return to it and renew ourselves of it regularly, especially if we are to be serious about living as co-hosts.

For faith communities and the faithful, this renewal is engaged via our personal and public worship. Worship consists of acts we participate in that brings us before God to remind us of what life is truly about. In this, we ought not to speak of what we 'get out' of it, but rather about getting better at it.

Worship is essentially a longing and response of the heart, independent of special abilities or capacities so that all—children, aged, sick and divergent—can, in their own way, come before God who hosts them towards safety, wholeness and mission.

Worship is participation, not consumption. It calls us to give up our notions of time, significance, and self-importance. It is a lowering of sorts as we humble ourselves before God to then have Him lift us up and send us out! Worship rehomes us towards our true human worth and glory, which is to co-host with God towards a kingdom where life is celebrated and generated.

Right worship leads us to rediscover the traditional Christian notion of Common Good—to bring forth what is true, good and beautiful in our lives and our world. It helps us understand ourselves as belonging to God and called to co-host with him. It is a call towards a stance of hospitality where we make sacrifices for another and trust that a greater good emerges as we create space and enjoin with the joys and sorrows of others.

This is of course challenging and unnerving as differences and at times outright conflicts mark our relationships. Thus, true worship begins as a subversive act that exposes our self-serving and self-preserving tendencies. These are points when the inward choices of the heart determine trajectories, and only a heart humbled in worship can choose the way that contributes to each other's flourishing.

Disciplined worship is the great enabling force that leads us to tap into flow of grace and love given to us in Christ, that charges us to turn toward one another rather than away.

Scripture addresses these realities plainly and aids us with simple instructions to take responsibility for our ruminations and expressions:

> *Instead, be kind to each other, tender-hearted, forgiving one another, just as God through Christ has forgiven you. (Ephesians 4:32 NLT)*

> *Fix your thoughts on what is true, and honourable, and right, and pure, and lovely, and admirable. Think about things that are excellent and worthy of praise. (Philippians 4:8 NLT)*

> *But now is the time to get rid of anger, rage, malicious behaviour, slander, and dirty language. Don't lie to each other, for you have stripped off your old sinful nature and all its wicked deeds. 10 Put on your new nature, and be renewed as you learn to know your Creator and become like him. (Colossians 3:8–10 NLT)*

These counsels call us to do three hospitable acts. Firstly, we are to protect and defend our relationship from destabilization by showing up and being willing to be stretched beyond our comfort zone. Second, as an intentional community, we must develop protocols for resolution, restitution and restoration as well as a process for discernment. This in turn calls for leadership that holds space, is patient and works diligently at issues of the heart.

The cultural winds that blow are fierce and persistent and the values of scientism and consumerism infiltrate faith and her institutions. The average local church is often adrift in the same waters, unable to lead her people to their identity of rest and power. Very often, the church is held hostage by the values of the world and imposes her version of success on guests and members alike, creating the burden for them to be a certain version of themselves, and to have to negotiate the rules of acceptance.

In contrast, the vision of the city where God's way of gracious hospitality reigns is rendered tenderly by the prophet Isaiah from the sixth century:

> *And the wolf will dwell with the lamb,*
> *And the leopard will lie down with the young goat,*
> *And the calf and the young lion and the fatling together;*
> *And a little boy will lead them.*
> *Also the cow and the bear will graze,*
> *Their young will lie down together,*
> *And the lion will eat straw like the ox. (Isaiah 11:6–7, NASB)*

Jesus' expands on this surprise where mortal enemies are able to feel safe together-

> *And they will come from east and west and from north*
> *and south, and will recline at the table in the kingdom*
> *of God. And behold, some are last who will be first*
> *and some are first who will be last." (Luke 13, NASB)*

All usual distinctions and demarcations come crumbling down and our usual expectations and understandings are turned on their heads. The unlikely and the impossible happens.

The City of God is a time-space reality where life thrives and humans flourish. It is filled with communities that welcome and enjoy the hospitality of God. It implies a real relationship among those who are different, and the willingness to be moved out of our comfort zone to be transformed in encounters where God is the ultimate Host.

The citizens in it believe that God extends, to all humankind, a divine and inexhaustible welcome in the transforming experience of hospitality, where the door is always open, the table always set, the arms always flung wide and outstretched. This is markedly different and contrasts with our usual experiences of life in a bustling city where we feel hurried and harried, a sense of home-lessness often pervading our soul.

This is the urgent need of our time, when even families be-come polarized by ideological differences. The only way to avoid the dismembering that such conflicts tend to cause is to hold space, encourage dialogue and listen deeply without *a priori* judgment. This requires us to stop seeing someone else as antagonistically different to us, but essentially like us.

This is what happened to a few young adults who encoun-tered wheelchair bound Chiew.

Singapore is a modern city-state with a reputation for our cleanliness, orderliness and efficiency. But we have an underbelly of people who are deeply marginalized. Chiew is one of them. As his mother did not carry an ID, Chiew was registered as a stateless persona non grata. This had a huge impact on his life.

> "I am stateless. When I became older, I was able to obtain a blue Permanent Resident (PR) Identification Card that lists my nationality as 'Unknown'. Although I have a PR status, I am still a stateless person. I have no passport and have never travelled out of the country. Despite be-ing born and raised here all my life, I have no place to call home."[1]

Chiew grew up mostly on the streets with his mom as his father would turn violent on occasions. They earned money by washing milk tins for reuse and often slept under heavy vehicles to be shaded from the sun when they were tired. On one occasion, the pair were so sound asleep that they did not notice the vehicle rumbling to life. As it moved, it ran over and broke one of Chiew's mom's toe.

Yet God's grace flowed to Chiew and his mom. There were kind souls who would offer suggestions in the form of a better place to wash the tins other than the dirty public toilet. The lorry uncle who handed them a hundred dollars. The pastor who was willing to organize his father's funeral and reached out persistently

---

1. Chiew's story is documented in biography here: https://homeless.sg/getupandgo/.

to the pair. The friend who took them into her one-room flat and the young adults who formed a life group to support them.

It can be said that in his need, Chiew also hosted these young adults—drawing them close to learn to become safe persons, to stretch in their view and use of life. They did not anticipate Chiew to be illiterate as literacy rates in Singapore are extremely high. When planning their routes, they would whip out their smartphones and use an app, so most were shocked to find out that Chiew often got lost as he could not read the street signs. This helped the young adults to see a whole new reality and learnt gratitude for what they took for granted.

True hospitality means that the guest and the host play dialogical roles that can switch, like a Mobius strip. Jesus had some friends who were special to him: three siblings named Lazarus, Mary and Martha. Per Middle Eastern practice, when Jesus visits them there would be a flurry of preparations. The gospel writer Luke recounts how Martha got frustrated when her sister Mary sat by Jesus to listen to him instead of helping her with the food preparations.[2]

She felt safe enough to express her frustration to Jesus. Surprisingly, he responded by saying that Mary had chosen the 'better portion'[3]. The words Jesus used indicated that He saw himself as the host who had brought choice and fitting portions for His guests.

Hence, while Jesus arrived as a guest and graciously accepted the hospitality of the siblings, He was also the host who offered food that only He could bring. Jesus gently reminded Martha that her hospitality needed to flow from tasting God's.

As Jesus was preparing His disciples for the new reality of the Kingdom of God, He told them on His last night with them to enact a ritual at the meal table. Through the Eucharist, Jesus helped them see that the transformation of life is not found primarily in heroic acts or mystical heights, but via the daily, ordinary and

2. Luke 10:38–41.
3. Luke 10:42.

needed activity of eating, drinking and being with others. Jesus gave the meal a whole new constitution as he took the bread and cup, gave thanks, and shared it. These three motions shape the life of faith. This is the Christian way to eat: accept your meal with thanks, delight in it, and then make sure your neighbor, be she in the next seat or on the street corner, has enough in her bowl too. Break the bread, give thanks and give it away.

To look at things this way is to look at them totally out of love and delight and aside from use, because God, the all-sufficient and totally complete, has no use for anything. We are to understand that He creates and enjoys, out of sheer effusive delight. When we look at a meal with the eyes of God, we point to each thing—the cosmic forces, creatures that have contributed to our spread, and the whole wide world— then turn to look at those around the table and say "Yes, this is good, and it is good that you are here".

> *And when He had taken some bread and given thanks, He broke it and gave it to them, saying,*
> *"This is My body which is given for you; do this in remembrance of Me. (Luke 22:19)*

Part 6 Highlights

- Our lives share common needs and are intertwined so we can learn to focus on our shared humanity and choose to impact each other for good.

- We cannot really live when we are cut off from God who is the Source of life and the ground of our being.

- We can reimagine our homes and interactions as spaces where we co-host with God.

- This is a radical new way to live that needs to be sustained with regular, committed personal and public worship.

- God has inaugurated His Kingdom, a new way of life, and we can partake and participate in it.

Soak & Savor

- Read the scenario Jesus painted about the judgment at the end of time. Can you see that He is calling us to admit that we all have the same needs, and are called to meet them for each other?

- How can you be a co-host where you reside, work and engage?

- Why is worship so central to this new way of living?

- Imagine a typical scenario in your life, where God is the host, and you are being invited to co-host with Him. How may this shape how you show up and respond?

Epilogue

I have only had a singular experience of the season of Fall. I live by the equator and our seasons consist of hot and hotter with torrential rains towards the end of the year. But the year I was in Minnesota, a new friend and I were musing about the great Mississippi river and wondered out loud where it all began. Although she was from the United States, she had not seen it either. We reached out to one other fellow-writer and soon we were the 'intrepid explorers' on a road trip to find where it all began for the Mississippi.

That year, Fall was a little late so where I was staying at that point, the leaves were not exactly glowing with the splendor of the season as I had hoped. But the drive northwards would change all of that.

After a couple of hours on the road, we arrived at Lake Itasca State Park. We browsed the museum and were astounded that this great river that flows all the way down to Mexico began in this small glacial lake, approximately 1.8 square miles in area. In fact, geologists believe that the lake itself is fed by smaller rivulets that can be considered the true origin of the river.

Perhaps God's love and grace which we experience as trickles will grow and gain momentum in our lives too and flow on forward to reach and water distant hearts.

Without proper shoes, I sat and waited as my friends took on a trail. When they returned, we walked in the woods around, a reverence filling us even as the silence was broken by the intermittent sounds of crushed leaves and gravel beneath our feet. We were surrounded by glorious bursts of yellows and orange as if happiness was taking on concrete form. My breath was swept away by the evocative and mesmerizing power of such raw beauty. I felt enveloped by it and drawn to step right into it and be lost in it. Unlike staring at a painting or watching a video, this was embedding, almost being swallowed up by raw beauty. I recall the words of Michael Fryer that "beauty is not some vague, abstract idea. It's the opposite... when there is a dearth of hope, beauty in all its forms, can create moments of transcendence."[1].

Many of us who can travel endure hours on the road to witness such vistas. We try to capture, interpret and even convey our experiences with photos, songs and stories. Life according to humans is the technological manipulation of nature for our ends: to enjoy ease, pleasure and productivity.

But in truth, beauty serves to lead us towards the Beautiful One if we pay attention. It is awakening our senses and calling forth our imagination to encounter God.

The encounter with God as Beautiful and hospitable may require going on a journey through your own soul's many twists and turns, through loving, being loved, hurting and being hurt in God's family. It can involve seasons and stations, starting and stopping, losses, gains, suffering and resurrection.

As I just stood there, dwarfed by the red and white pines, I entered a still point where I felt Someone embracing me. The leaves, at times swaying when the breeze came and often free-falling to the ground, made me feel like I had entered a happy, eternal dance. My soul felt like it was soaring, lifted to a horizon far beyond and above everything around me.

God created us out of freedom, to freely live and love. This is permanently lost to us as long as we continue to believe that life is for us to use up. But when we slowly respond to God's intimations of love and grace, intentionally seek out and develop our taste for His gracious hospitality, we will be led to springs and grandeur-charged moments of transformation which will shift us towards abundance and freedom.

---

1. Michael Fryer, "The Subversive Power of Beauty," *On Being*, March 2015.

In Psalm 27, the famous king David wrote of how he was facing enemies about him and expressed the sense of aloneness and abandonment he felt. Yet he maintained an equanimity as he made his way to sit and gaze at God's beauty in the temple. David was not attending to religion; he was tending to his soul's source by ceasing from the strife to find the safety he needed.

> *"One thing I ask from the Lord,*
>   *this only do I seek:*
> *that I may dwell in the house of the Lord*
>   *all the days of my life,*
> *to gaze on the beauty of the Lord*
>   *and to seek him in his temple."*

From this place of choice to sit and savor God's beauty, to experience that God is desirable, and that he is desired, David regained a right sense of priority, proportion and timing. As a result, he was able in the face of the harsh realities to declare:

> *The Lord is my light and my salvation—*
>   *whom shall I fear?*
> *The Lord is the stronghold of my life—*
>   *of whom shall I be afraid?*
> *For in the day of trouble*
>   *he will keep me safe in his dwelling;*
> *he will hide me in the shelter of his sacred tent*
>   *and set me high upon a rock.*

David found the headwaters.

The Poets

Desmond Francis Xavier Kon Zhicheng-Mingdé has authored nineteen books, spanning various genres. A former journalist, he has also edited over twenty-five titles. He can be found at: desmondkon.com

Jonathan Chan is a writer and editor. Born in New York to a Malaysian father and South Korean mother, he was raised in Singapore and educated at Cambridge and Yale universities. He is the author of poetry collection Going Home (Landmark, 2022) and Managing Editor of Poetry.Sg. More of his writing can be found at jonbcy.wordpress.com.

Nicole Ann Law is a Catholic podcaster with a love for storytelling. Her repertoire ranges from short prose and poetry to multiple podcasts to amplify His Glory. Focused on bringing His human face to others through real stories of struggle and hope, Nicole gently leads her audience into reflecting and looking inward to move forward (@nourishthesoul on Spotify)

Eric Tinsay Valles has published the poetry collections A World in Transit and After the Fall: dirges among ruins, as well as co-edited the Get Lucky Anthology of Singapore and Philippine Writings, Sg Poems 2015–2016, The Nature of Poetry, etc. He has won a Goh Sin Tub Creative Writing prize as well as the Illumination Award. You can read him in many places including on the Atelier of healing: poems about trauma and healing.

Aaron Lee is a bivocational pastor, ethics lawyer, writer-poet and cultural worker. He and his wife Namiko Chan Takahashi co-founded the Laniakea Culture Collective, an interdisciplinary art practice www.laniakea.la.

References

Allison, Dale C., *Encountering Mystery : Religious Experience in a Secular Age*. Grand Rapids, Michigan: William B. Eerdmans Publishing Company, 2022.

Bass, Dorothy C. *Receiving the Day: Christian Practices for Opening the Gift of Time*, Josey-Bass, 2000.

Bass, Dorothy C., Cahalan, Kathleen A., Miller-McLemore, Bonnie J., Nieman, James R., Scharen, *Christian B. Christian Practical Wisdom*. Eerdmans Publishing 2016.

Bretherton, Luke. *Hospitality as Holiness, Christian witness amid moral diversity*, Ashgate, Surrey, 2006.

Brueggemann, Walter, *The Land: Place as Gift, Promise and Challenge in Biblical Faith*. Fortress Press, 1977.

Byrne, Brendan. *The Hospitality of God : A Reading of Luke's Gospel*, Liturgical Press, 2000.

Colegate, Isabel, *A Pelican in the Wilderness: hermits, solitaries and recluses*, Washington D.C., Counterpoint, 2002.

Dinesh, Isak, *Seven Gothic Tales*, Knopf Doubleday Publishing Group, 1991.

Ekblad, Bob. *Reading the Bible with the Damned*. John Knox Press, 2005.

Elkington, Rob. *Visionary Leadership in a turbulent world*, ed. Jennifer Moss Breen, Rob Elkington, Madeleine Van Der Steege & Judith Glick-Smith, Emerald Publishing, 2017.

Elton, Terri Martinson, *Journeying in the wilderness: forming faith in the 21st century*. Minneapolis : Fortress Press, 2020.

Frankl, Viktor, *Man's Search for Meaning: An Introduction to Logotherapy*; Simon and Shuster, 1984.

Gruen, Anselm. *Heaven Begins Within You: wisdom from the desert fathers*. New York.: Croesroad Publishing, 1999.

Halverson, Delia. *The Gift of Hospitality, in church, in the home, in all of life*. Chalice Press, Missouri, 1999.

Hershberger, Michele. *A Christian View of Hospitality, expecting surprises*. Herald Press, Pennsylvania, 1999.

Jethani, Skye. *The Divine Commodity: Discovering a Faith Beyond Consumer Christianity*. Zondervan, 2013.

Jipp, Joshua W. *Saved by Faith and Hospitality*. William B. Eerdmans Publishing, Michigan, 2017.

References

Jones, E. Stanely. *The Unshakable Kingdom and the Unchanging Person*. McNett Press, 1995.

Karl, Rahner. *Theological Investigations VII*, New York: Seabury Press 1972.

Kirk, David. "Hospitality: Essence of Eastern Christian Lifestyle", *Diakonia* 16/2 (1981): 112.

Kleespie, Nicholas O.S.B. *Mission of Hospitality*. Abbey Banner. St John's Abbey, Spring 2022.

Kram, Gabriel Natureva. *Restorative Practices: of Wellbeing: A Compendium of Restorative Practices*. Jaguar Imprint, 2020.

Luke, T. Johnson, *Sharing Possessions*. Fortress Press, 1981.

McIntyre, Mike. *The Kindness of Strangers: Penniless Across American*. New York: Berkeley Books, 1996.

Newman, Elizabeth. *Untamed hospitality: welcoming God and other strangers*. Grand Rapids, Mich.: Brazos Press, 2007.

Nouwen, Henri, *Reaching Out*. New York, Image, 1975.

Pohl, Christine D. *Making room: recovering hospitality as a Christian tradition*. Grand Rapids, Mich.: W.B. Eerdmans, 1999.

Richard, Lucien. *Living the hospitality of God*, New York: Paulist Press, 2000.

Russell, Letty M. ed. Shannon Clarkson and Kate M. Ott, *Just Hospitality, God's Welcome in a World of Difference*. John Knox Press 2009.

Robinson, Marilynne. *Housekeeping*. New York, Picador, 1980.

Ross, Maggie. *Seasons of death and life: a wilderness memoir*. 1st ed. San Francisco: Harper, 1990.

Saunders, George. *A Swim in a Pond in the Rain*. New York: Random House, 2021.

Smith, James K.A. *Desiring the Kingdom: Worship, Worldview, and Cultural Formation (Cultural Liturgies)*. Baker Academic, 2009.

Sutherland, Arthur. *I was a stranger: a Christian Theology of Hospitality*. Abingdon Press, Nashville, 2006.

Taylor, Brian C. *Spirituality for Everyday Living, an adaptation of the Rule of St. Benedict*. Collegeville, MN.: Liturgical Press, 1989.

Taylor, Charles. *Sources of The Self. The Making of the Modern Identity*. Massachusetts, Havard University Press, 1989.

Tomaine, Jane. *St Benedict's Toolbox. The nuts and bolts of everyday Benedictine living*. Pennsylvania, Morehouse Publishing 2005.

Turner, Victor. *The Ritual Process*. New York: Cornell University Press, 1969.

Walters, Kerry S. *Soul Wilderness: A Desert Spirituality*. New York: Paulist Press, 2001.

Wrobleski, Jessica. *The Limits of Hospitality*. Collegeville, Minn.: Liturgical Press, 2012.

Online Resources

Articles and Essays

To Be a Guest. What Jesus, Odysseus, and African tradition teach about how to receive hospitality. By Emma Newgarden, The Plough

REFERENCES

"My peace I give to you": Ronald Knox on the Eucharist and the gift of peace on Catholic World Report.

How Much Data Do We Create Every Day? The Mind-Blowing Stats Everyone Should Read by Bernard Marr on Forbes.com

The Story of https://homeless.sg/getupandgo/ - story of Wong Hui Chiew, homeless.sg

The Subversive Power of Beauty. Michael Fryer, On Being (March 2015)

Butter Salted Transcendence by Nathan Beacom on Ekstasis Magazine.

How Many Thoughts Do You Have Each Day? And Other Things to Think About by Crystal Raypole. medically reviewed by Jacquelyn Johnson, PsyD, February 28, 2022

Sacred Spaces: Mother Teresa on seeking out the lonely in our midst by Moira Cullen, Ann Arbor. Com, 2011

Welcoming Spring: Hildegard on "viriditas" and the greening of the soul, by Almut Furchert in CloisterSeminars.org

Music 'He didn't life us up to let us down' by The Imperials in Heed the Call. (c) Webinars

Thompson, Curt and Dudiak, Jeff. Neurobiology and the Soul, The Trinity Forum. Webinar, June 24, 2022